W9-BSJ-237

Donald Davie

Wheaton 10.12.84

A Gathered Church

By the same author

Collected Poems 1950–1970
Thomas Hardy and British Poetry
The Shires

DONALD DAVIE

The Clark Lectures 1976

A Gathered Church

THE LITERATURE OF THE ENGLISH DISSENTING INTEREST, 1700–1930

Oxford University Press
New York
1978

Published 1978 in the United States of America by
Oxford University Press, Inc.
200 Madison Avenue,
New York,
N.Y. 10016

First published in Great Britain in 1978
by Routledge & Kegan Paul Ltd.

© Donald Davie 1978

Library of Congress Cataloging in Publication Data

Davie, Donald.
A gathered church.
(The Clark lectures; 1976)
1. Dissenters, Religious – England – Addresses, essays, lectures.
2. Dissenters – England – Addresses, essays, lectures.
3. England – Church history.
I. Title.
II. Series: The Clark lectures,
Trinity College, Cambridge University; 1976.
BX5201.D38   1978   274.1   77-12110
ISBN 0-19-519999-5

All Rights Reserved. No part of this publication
may be reproduced or transmitted in any form
or by any means, electronic or mechanical,
including photocopy, recording or any
information storage and retrieval system,
without permission in writing from the
publishers

Printed in Great Britain

There are so few people now who want to have any intimate spiritual association with the eighteenth and nineteenth centuries: . . . who bothers at all now about the work and achievement of our grandfathers, and how much of what they knew have we already forgotten?
DIETRICH BONHOEFFER, *Letters and Papers from Prison*

It is certain, that the latitudinarian and the fanatic mutually prepare proselytes for each other. . . . The repeated admonitions that have been given to parents, to avoid making their children bigots, or teaching them mysteries before their reason ripened, has caused young people to be trained up in such ignorance of the faith which they profess, as would have astonished every age since the Reformation. To this, I am persuaded, we must ascribe the recent progress of Calvinism. . . .
MRS WEST, *Letters to a Young Lady*

It was not politics that produced Nonconformity, and it is not politics that can perfect it. If an Established Church were the clear will of Christ, any sense of political injustice would have to be educated into submission. The question is a religious one, and must be settled on religious principles.
P. T. FORSYTH, *The Charter of the Church*

Contents

Illustrations

The Nonconformist Contribution
to English Culture

IF ANYONE THINKS that the title of this series of lectures seems demure, the presumptuous title of this first one ought to disabuse him. And I should like to explain. . . . Thirty-six years ago, when I came up to this university as a freshman from the West Riding, I was happy to join the Robert Hall Society, which I am glad to know still flourishes (or at any rate persists) as the association for Baptists in the university. At the same time I was – and not reluctantly either, but with enthusiasm – studying for the English Tripos. How did those two allegiances come together, to define the sort of Englishman that I was, or wanted to be? This wasn't a question which at that time agitated me much, chiefly because my Baptist allegiance was already by then lukewarm. Over the years, however, the question has interested me a good deal, and in these lectures I want to sketch the answer that I have found to it. It is not a straightforward answer, but nuanced and elusive; so much so, that I've decided the only practical way of conveying it is by sketching the fortunes of English Dissent over the last 280 years.

And 'sketch' of course is the best it can be; yet, sketchy or not, I hope it will give me opportunities for clearing the English dissenting tradition of various libels that circulate about it. Accordingly it is not too soon for me to make it plain that I speak no longer as a Baptist, nor indeed from within the ranks of Dissent at all. To that extent I can claim to be impartial. More-over, since what we are concerned with is English *culture*, our history cannot be a history of ideas, nor a history of events, nor

1

yet a narrowly *literary* history, but a history of people and the styles in which they lived – a history, therefore, which, whenever I can manage it, shall incorporate thumbnail biographies.

We may begin by taking note of Sir Ernest Barker declaring, in his *Britain and the British People* (1942): 'Apart from any question of their relative numerical strength, it may be said that the general relations, the general balance, and the general interaction of Anglicanism and Nonconformity have been a cardinal factor in English life and development for over three centuries.' And we may set beside that G. M. Trevelyan deciding, in *An Autobiography* (1949): 'from the Restoration to the later years of the Nineteenth Century, the continuity of the two parties in English politics was very largely due to the two-party system in religious observance, popularly known as Church and Chapel.' It will hardly be contested that among literary historians of the last three centuries in England we look in vain for anything that parallels these assertions by distinguished social and political historians like Barker and Trevelyan. 'Chapel' as against 'Church' isn't a distinction that our literary historians have found much use for, though their colleagues in social history and political history have found it indispensable. How can this be?

In an introductory lecture some painting in bold strokes may be permitted. And in this spirit we may venture a broad and facile reply to the question just raised: 'Chapel', it may be said, fails to figure in literary history as crucially as in social and political history, precisely because literature, and the creative and performing arts in general, are just what 'Chapel' distrusts, if indeed it does not positively condemn them. This is a commonly received notion; for what is the dissenter ('the nonconformist') if not the heir of those Cromwellian Roundheads who defaced the icons of our cathedrals and parish churches? The chapel-goer is the iconoclast, by origin and by definition; the literary *ikon*, no less than the painted or the carved ('graven images'), is what he is committed to destroying, or to tolerating only on unacceptably restrictive and emasculating terms – and in this way the 'Chapel' interest does indeed play a crucial and momentous part in the literary history of England, as 'the enemy', as precisely that which, in each generation, English artists must do battle with, and circumvent as best they can. On this showing, you perceive, that my situation all those years ago – as a young Baptist in love with English poetry, and determined to write poems himself – was quite simply anomalous, self-contradictory.

But that view of the matter does not square with my experience, nor is it borne out by the historical record. In particular it does not square with our records of England in the early eighteenth century. Ian Watt showed this twenty years ago, in relation to one dissenter of that period, Daniel Defoe. In my next lecture I shall argue a similar case, in relation to one of Defoe's contemporaries, a rather different sort of dissenter, the poet Isaac Watts (1674–1748). When I began studying Watts closely some years ago, I found (if I may quote myself) that:

> the curiously ambiguous status of Watts as poet – his figuring modestly in all respectable anthologies and a great deal more largely in our oral tradition, yet never remembered as one in the succession of our illustrious poets – reflects, one cannot help but think, a similar ambiguity in the official or received version of English culture when it comes to assessing the contribution to that culture of puritanism in general and of nonconformists in particular.

And I observed in print, with some indignation: 'One looks in vain for any general recognition that the artistic culture of the nation, so far from being repudiated by nonconformists as the product of a ruling class or an alien caste, has been embraced by the best of them in every generation, and enriched (though also at times valuably purged) by their efforts.' I now think this was excessive. Distinguished individuals from the ranks of Dissent have indeed enriched our culture in every generation since 1700, but Dissent as such, as a corporate force in our society, can at a certain point be shown to have ceased to do so. And in so far as I shall have to show this, the story I have to tell is a sad one.

Two misunderstandings can be cleared up, or at any rate indicated, here and now, for they arise from two words in what I have just quoted from myself – the words 'puritanism' and 'culture'. First, 'culture'. . . . It should be clear that I am using this word in a restricted sense, which is nowadays old-fashioned. I am supposing that at or very near the centre of what we take 'culture' to mean, there is the practice and appreciation of the traditionally fine arts, of certain performing arts, and certain crafts; also the practice and appreciation of free speculation, philosophical in the full sense, including that *natural* philosophy which we call 'science'. Everyone knows that there is current a quite different usage, by which 'culture' is defined and diagnosed far more as a matter of social and political organization, and of patterns of social and political behaviour. In this second sense of the word, the culture of English Dissent has been studied exhaustively and respectfully, though also at times tendentiously; to the names of Ernest Barker and G. M. Trevelyan we may add the names of (among a multitude of others) Elie Halévy, Eric Hobsbawm, E. P. Thompson. It's precisely because Dissent has been looked at from this point of view so often, that I have thought it may be interesting and useful to look at it through a more old-fashioned pair of spectacles. However, it would be foolish to think that these two meanings for 'culture' are mutually exclusive; on the contrary we may be sure that these two meanings overlap and slide into each other – the arts and speculations of a culture (or of a sub-culture, such as we may take English Dissent to be) are intimately related to the patterns of social behaviour in that sub-culture. On the other hand we too seldom acknowledge that these interrelations, though they certainly exist, are still, as they always have been, too subtle and intricate for our historical scholarship to draw them out with any confidence. And in my third lecture, when I'll be concerned with the very special sort of Dissent which we call Wesleyanism, I shall take note of what I take to be an illegitimate transition, from Wesleyanism considered as a pattern of social and political behaviour to the body of literary art which Wesleyanism produced – that is to say, the hymns of Charles Wesley.

Moreover, religious belief and religious observance are themselves cultural phenomena, and from yet a third point of view may be seen as more central to 'culture' than either the aesthetic tastes and achievements which chiefly interest me, or the social behaviour-patterns which interest, for instance, E. P. Thompson.

Charles Wesley, if he returned to earth, would presumably be not much less bored and impatient with my interest in examining his hymns as poems, than with Thompson's examining them to see if they helped or hindered the social consciousness of the English working class. Either interest, he would feel, was an evasion of what was for him the central concern – Salvation. The last literary man to try to grapple with this awkward fact – that religious experience is a momentous and determining feature of culture – was T. S. Eliot, in books like *After Strange Gods* and *Notes Towards the Definition of Culture* and *The Idea of a Christian Society*. I go along with the consensus of opinion, in thinking that these are among Eliot's least satisfactory works; but I'm inclined to think that they are unsatisfactory because of the intractability of the issues to which Eliot addressed himself, at least as much as because of any slackness or self-indulgence in Eliot himself. I have tried to avoid this intractable territory as carefully as, from his different point of view, E. P. Thompson has. But neither of us has been wholly successful. And we all need to acknowledge, and remind ourselves, that the thorny issue exists. To be specific: when in April 1796 the Baptist minister in Norwich, Mark Wilks, preached two 'Jacobin Collection Sermons' to defray the expenses of the legal defence of John Horne Tooke and John Thelwall, Professor Thompson takes it for granted that this was a culturally enlightened and enlightening thing to do. My own verdict on it would have to await an examination whether, given the occasion and the circumstances, Mark Wilks's use of English testified to lively and flexible responsiveness in him and in his milieu. But to Charles Wesley or T. S. Eliot – both of them, as it happens, High Tories – the question might well be whether Mark Wilks did not fail in his pastoral duties by impeding the devotions of those of his flock who happened to hold strong sentiments in favour of the king and the *status quo*. According as we hold by the first or the second or the third understanding of 'culture', our judgment of a cultural phenomenon like Mark Wilks's two sermons will differ.

As for the second of our problematic words, 'puritanism', it must be clear that this is by no means synonymous with either 'nonconformity' or 'Dissent' – two words that for the moment may be treated as interchangeable, though there are circumstances in which they are not so. 'Puritanism' is not a phenomenon that is encountered only among the dissenting sects. Since 1700, as before that also, a remarkable number of the most devoted Puritans and iconoclasts have been in fact members of the Established Church. Augustus Toplady may serve as one example out of many: author of 'Rock of Ages', bitterly Calvinist opponent of John Wesley's Arminianism, yet himself a priest of the Church of England. As was John Wesley himself! If Wesleyanism was a Puritan movement, as in some sense it surely was, it took its rise and ran its course, so long as the Wesley brothers were alive, inside the Church of England. The same is true, after the Wesleys were dead, of the Evangelical Movement, recognizably the source of most of the allegedly 'life-denying' Puritanism that we see our Victorian writers contending with. Though there *were* dissenting Evangelicals, the justly famous or notorious Clapham Sect – the powerhouse of Evangelicalism – was Anglican. Henry Thornton, William Wilberforce, Charles Grant, Lord Teignmouth, Zachary Macaulay, James Stephen – all were members of the Established Church. And it is these, the notabilities of the Clapham Sect, whose Puritanism engenders by reaction, two generations later, the calculated libertinism and deviance of their brilliant progeny whom we may agree to describe as 'Bloomsbury'; a positively theatrical reversal, of which the poetic justice has been delineated here in Cambridge – quite properly, since Cambridge was the forcing house in which English Puritanism flowered into such a prodigious blossom as Lytton Strachey. But this – the at once genetic and cultural logic by which Virginia Woolf and Vanessa Bell spring from the loins of James Stephen, and E. M. Forster comes of the stock of Marianne Thornton – though it is certainly a lurid and instructive chapter in the history of English Puritanism, has nothing immediately to do with the history (literary, social, political, or whatever) of nonconformity, of the English 'dissenting interest'. Evangelicalism is one thing. Puritanism is something else. What we are concerned with is *Dissent*. In my last lecture indeed I shall suggest that when D. H. Lawrence in this century challenges and assails 'Bloomsbury', we see the heir to the dissenting conscience at odds with the heirs to the Evangelical conscience – but with this melancholy qualification, that by the time of this showdown the one ethos is as far gone in decrepitude as the other. Since both parties to this dispute had suffered the evaporation of that which originally fuelled both of them – that is to say, Christian belief – neither of them offers a coherent or selfconsistent ideology; and hence, it may well seem, the conflict between them hardly deserves the pother that it has provoked, and continues to provoke, among us.

There is of course one literary masterpiece of English Dissent which cannot escape the attention of even the idlest undergraduate reading for the English Tripos: *The Pilgrim's Progress*! Certainly *I* knew Bunyan's great book, and knew that it was 'a classic', long before I came up to St Catharine's – knew it not from my schoolmasters either, but from the exiguous library of my grandfather, Baptist deacon and lay-preacher. Alas, it was long after the Tripos had come and gone that I applied myself to the atrociously printed edition of *The Pilgrim's Progress* that came to me off his shelves, and there discovered – because the edition was designed and annotated as a book of devotion for the pious, not as an ornament of 'English Literature' – that over and above Bunyan's humanity and his raciness and his humour and everything that makes him a proto-novelist, there was a rigorously consistent intellectual armature to the whole of his narrative, the intricately and impressively logical structure of the Calvinist scheme of salvation. Things change, not always for the worse; and so I'm prepared to believe that it's now impossible to study Bunyan's book in the university without studying Calvinist theology also. But I put it on record that it was abundantly possible, thirty-six years ago.

In any case, what happened, once Bunyan was dead, to the England that John Bunyan stood for? Did that Calvinist England achieve cultural respectability just once, once and for all, in *The Pilgrim's Progress* and *Grace Abounding*? Was the story, from

then on, all downhill? Was it indeed worse than that? Did the
Englishman that John Bunyan stood for and spoke for become
thereafter a grotesque, a comical though also sinister bogey-man,
a bigot and an obscurantist, whose role in the arts and the speculative thought of England was thereafter as 'the enemy'? Here in
another form is that same question which I was too harried or too
timid to confront all those years ago, to which I address myself
now.

Whichever way one comes at it, one has to contend with one's
own ignorance. Certainly this is true if one's education has been
literary, as mine was. One does not have to read very far to discover how disabled we are, as literary historians, by our custom-
ary ignorance of theology and church history. One egregious
error, for instance, I slipped into my last paragraph, when I spoke
of Bunyan's England as 'that Calvinist England', quite as if
Calvinism were a monopoly of the dissenting churches. Yet in
1773 in the House of Lords, the elder Pitt, Earl of Chatham,
replied to Drummond, Archbishop of York:

> The Dissenting Ministers are represented as men of close ambition;
> they are so, my Lords; and their ambition is to keep close to the col-
> lege of fishermen, not of cardinals; and to the doctrines of inspired
> apostles, not to the decrees of interested and aspiring bishops. They
> contend for a scriptural and spiritual worship; we have a Calvinistic
> Creed, a Popish Liturgy and Arminian Clergy.

Here 'we' means 'we Anglicans', and so Pitt is saying that the
Creed in the *Book of Common Prayer* either is a Calvinist document or at all events is capable of being given a strictly Calvinist
interpretation. And of course this is manifestly true: the Calvinist
doctrine of election and (its fearsome corollary, which is the real
sticking-point) the doctrine of *reprobation* could be, and were,
preached from Anglican pulpits as often as in dissenting chapels.
Toplady was one who preached thus, and George Whitefield was
another. On the other hand, many dissenting ministers were
affronted by the doctrine of reprobation, and did their best to
alleviate it or to get round it. Even before Bunyan, the great
Richard Baxter attempted this, and evolved what the strict Calvinists through the next century, in Church and Chapel alike,

8

condemned as heretical 'Baxterianism'. Again, in his *Help to Zion's Travellers* (1781), Robert Hall the elder, a Baptist minister like his more famous son who ministered and is commemorated here in Cambridge, argued – with a linguistic nicety that must appeal to the literary man – that 'reprobation' is in Scripture opposed not to 'election' but to *approbation* (as of course propriety of usage would seem to require). Or again (most poignantly) there is the Anglican but rigorously Calvinist William Cowper. Which is the more characteristically Calvinist response – Cowper's seeing the solitude of Alexander Selkirk as the worst of all possible privations, or Defoe's Crusoe exulting in it, as the condition of his autonomy? In short, it is not on doctrinal issues that 'Chapel' divides off from 'Church', nor for the most part one dissenting sect from another. In nearly every communion including the Established Church could be found, at any given date, the full range of theological positions from the strictest Calvinism to Arminianism and indeed beyond; and the Wesleyan movement itself was from the start cleft down the middle, between the Arminianism of the Wesley brothers and the Calvinism of George Whitefield. Perhaps the most startling example of how little it was doctrine that held a communion together is the evolution in the eighteenth century of English Presbyterianism which, lacking the Establishment status that held Scottish Presbyterianism together, had by 1800 dissolved almost completely into Unitarianism – that is to say, from one point of view had removed itself outside the field of revealed religion altogether, and certainly to a point as far as possible from John Knox! The significance of this development is very great, and yet nowadays almost invariably overlooked; we shall need to return to it.

However, there is more to be said about John Bunyan. . . . The seventeenth century is the heroic age of English Dissent. Nothing is more common than to find it applauded thus, alike within and without the dissenting communions, indeed by infidels like Leslie Stephen as by believers. But in this there is a species of sentimentalism that is discreditable. To be plain about it, the scheme of salvation that Bunyan advances in *The Pilgrim's Progress* is, in its ferocious rigour, such as few Christians today – not to speak of unbelievers – can stomach; and is there not accordingly an unpleasant duplicity about applauding Bunyan for the humane feeling that he managed to express inside a framework inimical to it, without at least acknowledging the inhumanity of that frame? More certainly, there is an unpleasantness about extolling the heroically uncompromising consistency of the old Puritans when they maintained their doctrines in all their primitive ferocity, and then going on to speak sneeringly of temporizers and compromisers when one finds later dissenters who, sharing our sense of affront, attempt to modify doctrine so as to remove those stumbling blocks. This is how Leslie Stephen – himself safely outside the Christian fold, and watching from the sidelines – treats of the Baxterian compromise that Isaac Watts was trying for in the generation after Bunyan. Certainly the Puritanism of Bunyan and John Knox was 'grand'; it was also bigoted, ferocious and uncharitable. Perhaps the issue is at its clearest when Leslie Stephen writes of Burns:

> A hundred years before, Burns might have been a Covenanter and have met the shock of Claverhouse's troopers at Drumclog. But the old Covenanting spirit had become a thing of shreds and patches – an effete idol no longer capable of rallying true men to its side. And therefore Burns puts his whole heart into such tremendous satires as 'Holy Willie's Prayer'.

In its context, this carries the unmistakable implication that for Burns to have been a Covenanter would have been something very splendid and stirring. Had Walter Scott written *Old Mortality* in vain, that Stephen should thus warm to an image of Burns made over into the image of Balfour of Burleigh? There is a sort of *machismo* at work here – one notes the invocation of 'true men' ('capable of rallying true men to its side') – which is by no means dead among historians of Dissent at the present day, and which makes it certain that the enlightening and civilizing work for Dissent of such as Watts and Philip Doddridge and Job Orton, or of either of the two Robert Halls, will continue to be scouted as somehow effeminate and emasculating, and that commentators will be proud to admit to 'a sneaking respect' for such

a seventeenth-century survivor into Watts's day as Thomas Bradbury, his redoubtable opponent in the quarrels of early eighteenth-century Congregationalism. All one asks is that when
people confess to a 'sneaking respect', they give some weight to
the epithet; few of us would like to live with the Calvinist tenets of
election and reprobation in their primitive seventeenth-century
ferocity, and it is certainly 'sneaking' to think we can take over
the masculine force of that ideology without paying the price in
private terror and despair.

In 1710, it seemed to many that these bogeys had been laid to
rest once and for all, for Daniel Whitby, a Salisbury rector, in his
Discourse published that year, seemed to have dealt a death-blow
to the concept of predestination on which both doctrines rest; and
this was as welcome to enlightened dissenters as to middle-of-the-
road Anglicans. But fortunately or unfortunately there was a
seven-year-old boy then growing up on the frontier of the settle-
ments in North America, who would turn out to be a theologian
and logician of genius who could and did rebut Whitby and prove
that predestination and free will are compatible. This was the
great Jonathan Edwards, whose vindication of strict Calvinist
dogma was not to be published until 1754, as his *Careful and
Strict Enquiry into the Modern Prevailing Notions of Freedom of
Will*. But Edwards's thoughts had matured long before that, and
they may have been brought back to England as soon as George
Whitefield returned from his first evangelizing swing through the
American colonies in 1738, having preached in Edwards's
church in Northampton, Massachusetts. In any case, by the end
of the century Edwards's restatement of Calvinism in all its uncompromising rigour had so carried the day that his son could
point contemptuously to English Calvinists like Watts and
Doddridge as having been compelled to 'bow in the house of
Rimmon'.

To regret the emergence of this rejuvenated Calvinism may
look like the merest sentimentality, for after all if Edwards's
Calvinism was thought through and simply *true*, as Watts's
wasn't, should we not rejoice that the truth prevailed? It would
need a theologian to deal with that question. Edwards's doctrine,

as far as I can see, has never been controverted, and perhaps it is incontrovertible, but in the last hundred years it has for the most part been tacitly laid aside, as experimentally unacceptable to the worshipper in the act of private devotion or public worship. The strict Calvinist doctrinal system was never overthrown; and yet it has been very largely abandoned as offensive to *sensibility*. Is the same not true of other systems of ideas, in other fields – such as Robert Filmer's theory of a patriarchal monarchy? A question for historians of ideas! What seems certain is that this later history of strict Calvinism removes from Doddridge and Watts the reproach of being weakly genteel temporizers and compromisers; they apprehended the revulsion of sensibility, doubtless indeed they shared it, and they attempted to save Calvinism none the less by accepting Baxterian and other modifications. Perhaps unfortunately, Edwards's revitalizing of the logical rigour of the pure doctrine gave a new lease of life to it, through such as Whitefield and Toplady, and Evangelicalism generally after the deaths of the Wesleys.

I return to my point that an enthusiasm for *The Pilgrim's Progress*, and for seventeenth-century Puritanism in general, is likely to disqualify us from valuing eighteenth-century Dissent at the rate that it deserves. Bunyan's masterpiece is likely to arouse expectations; expectations of 'the heroic', such as later dissenting literature can only disappoint. And the same is true of that other, very different masterpiece of seventeenth-century Puritanism, *Paradise Lost*. In particular our sentimentalizing of the old Puritans takes a special turn when we call up an image of the ragged and humble congregations that Bunyan addressed in the fields of Bedfordshire. When we turn from that picture to the sleekly sober and wealthy congregation that Isaac Watts ministered to in London only a generation later, the shock is a severe one. And we are likely to jump to the conclusion that Dissent has 'sold out', that it has abandoned its natural and original constituency among those whom E. P. Thompson calls 'Christ's poor', and has settled hypocritically for the flesh-pots of the mercantile *bourgeoisie*. And yet most of us are familiar, if only sketchily, with the reasons why that explanation needn't be, and

probably isn't, the correct one. I have in mind the argument associated with the names of Max Weber and R. H. Tawney, which
proceeds by showing how many of the social practices applauded
and adopted by Puritanism – regularity, sobriety, frugality, and so
on – are practices which, other things being equal, lead to success
in the counting-house. One need go no further to explain how
often worldly and financial success came to those whose hopes
were set – so they would have said, and no doubt sincerely – on
another world altogether. To be sure, this argument is sus-
piciously neat and schematic; and an exhaustive demographic
survey of eighteenth-century dissenting congregations – something which I believe has never yet been attempted, and may
indeed be impossible – would doubtless blur the outlines very
greatly. It seems certain, for instance, that one must make a sharp
distinction between congregations in London and other centres of
commercial enterprise such as Bristol or King's Lynn, and congregations in the countryside. There is evidence that through to
the end of the century Dissent was drawing much of its strength
from artisans and mechanics in the towns, and from farm
labourers in the country. As late as 1830, if we may believe Mark
Rutherford in *The Revolution in Tanner's Lane*, there were to be
found in country towns congregations like the Baptist one he describes, whose minister was ignored by the Independent (i.e.
Congregational) minister, by the Wesleyan minister, and of
course by the rector – 'not because of any heresy or difference of
doctrine, but because he was a poor man and poor persons sat
under him'.

In any case, dissenters suffered under legal disabilities throughout the eighteenth-century. And their political disabilities may
well have helped their economic well-being, such as it was, for
their energies, arbitrarily shut out from government service and
from many of the professions, flowed the more strongly into the
channels of trade and finance. Nevertheless, all concessions and
dubieties allowed for, the contrast between Dissent in Bunyan's
lifetime and in Isaac Watts's remains stark. What had intervened
was the Revolutionary Settlement, which ensured the Protestant
succession; a constitutional guarantee which for the more restive

and suspicious dissenters was perfected only when, at the death of the last Stuart, Anne, the Hanoverian succession was assured. Thereafter, at least until the trouble with the American colonies, the house of Brunswick had no more loyal and zealous subjects than the dissenters, and the Whig hegemony no more reliable supporters. Politically disabled they might be, and would growl and protest about it, but mostly it seems they tolerated it readily enough as a price to be paid for getting protection from Papists, Jacobites and high-flying Tories. Thus, whereas the dissenters remained in tension with the national society both religiously and politically, that tension has been let down so notably since Bunyan's day, that 'accommodation' – that very unheroic process – may justly enough be seen as the characteristic endeavour and achievement of Dissent in the generations of Defoe and Watts and Doddridge. Accordingly, no one can be much further from the truth than was Helen Corke, D. H. Lawrence's friend, when she was commenting on a passage from Lawrence's *Apocalypse*. Lawrence had written: 'Every citizen is a unit of worldly power. A man may wish to be a pure Christian and a pure individual. But since he *must* be a member of some political State or nation, he is forced to be a unit of worldly power.' And Helen Corke comments: 'Ignorance of this plain fact was the prime error of early Nonconformity, and *The Pilgrim's Progress* was its most vocal expression. Eighteenth and nineteenth century Nonconformity walled itself round with a crude individual arrogance uglier than the walls of its ugly chapels.' On the contrary, there could be no clearer example of 'giving unto Caesar that which is Caesar's, and unto God that which is God's' than the unswerving devotion of the eighteenth-century dissenters to the Hanoverian dynasty, even though that dynasty continued to load them with civic disabilities. And as it happens eighteenth-century chapels were not uniformly, nor usually, 'ugly'. Such ignorance by twentieth-century dissenters of their own dissenting heritage is, I'm afraid, rather the rule than an exception.

What the dissenters accommodated to was 'bourgeois'? Well, to be sure! If we make any sense at all when we put 'bourgeois' along with 'culture' (and Raymond Williams for one has doubted

if we do), who has ever questioned that the culture of eighteenth-
century England was a bourgeois culture? Isaac Watts was bourgeois as Dr Johnson was, or Edward Gibbon, or even John
Wilkes. The term is descriptive, not pejorative; and in that sense
it may be doubted whether 'bourgeois' is not the word for the
culture that we have, which we study and presumably try to
preserve, from all the years between 1700 and the present day.
As I have explained, the dissenters' contribution to that common
culture is precisely what we are concerned with.

What needs to be said is that the romanticizing of seventeenth-
century Puritanism, which we have seen in Leslie Stephen, is not
a peculiarly Victorian vice, but is rife among us today. In fact,
through many decades now, it has taken a new turn, fuelled by
new motives and given a new polemical purpose. Our Left-wing
historians and opinion-makers have an obvious interest in extolling the Cromwellian republic and the intransigent or radical
Dissent which brought that republic into being and sustained it,
as also in censuring the Dissent which, once the Cromwellian
interregnum was over, sought an accommodation with the
restored monarchy, Stuart in the first place and Hanoverian later.
And accordingly we find the Master of Balliol, in one of his more
popularizing works (*Reformation to Industrial Revolution: A
Social and Economic History of Britain, 1530–1780*), declaring of
Dissent in the early eighteenth century: 'The cosmic battles
which Milton and Bunyan depicted were succeeded by sterile controversies over deism and unitarianism.' But of course, sterile is
as sterile does; a controversy will seem fruitless when the fruit
that it bears is such as you don't want and can't digest. If the fruit
that Christopher Hill had been looking for had been a more exact
grasp of doctrinal truth, and greater sincerity in religious worship, then eighteenth-century controversies about deism and unitarianism might seem even today to bear fruit that is wholesome
enough. For the moment we are not looking for that fruit any
more than Christopher Hill is; we are looking for something else
– for literature, and in particular, devotional poetry. And the
point to be made is simply that such poetry cannot get an un-
prejudiced scrutiny so long as the whole sub-culture from which

it springs is closed off from us by such a blanket condemnation as the one just quoted.

Nor does Christopher Hill leave it there; in the less than six pages which he devotes to 'Religion and Intellectual Life' in the eighteenth century, he finds room to declare (p. 231): 'The years of Walpole's rule, so peaceful, so prosperous, seem also to have been years of spiritual desolation as men contemplated the barren mechanical universe of Newton, and the new dismal science of economics which Mandeville took to its logical conclusion.' Who am I to demur when economics is called a 'dismal science'? Nor do I pretend that all these emphases can be laid at the door of Christopher Hill's Marxism; on the contrary, 'the barren mechanical universe of Newton' is a locution that I remember in my undergraduate years hearing from mouths that were impeccably High Church and Tory. Indeed, there is a curious un-animity on these matters which produces strange bed-fellows. We may set beside Christopher Hill's 'years of spiritual desolation', Father Ronald Knox, of all people, advising us in 1950: 'We need not doubt that the Evangelical movement had a powerful effect in waking up eighteenth-century England from its religious apathy, or that eighteenth-century England needed it.' But with all due deference to Christopher Hill and Ronald Knox alike, that is precisely what we *do* need to doubt! To give Leslie Stephen his due, he made this point very firmly (*History of English Thought in the Eighteenth Century*):

> It has become a common practice to denounce the frigidity and form-ality of the eighteenth century. . . . But I do not feel certain that we could mention in the first half of the nineteenth century three bishops whose characters make upon us a greater impression of purity and devotion than those of Berkeley, Butler, and Wilson; I doubt whether among those of less dignity we should find men more honest and manly than Clarke, or with a finer glow of devotional sentiment than William Law; and if the dissenters, freed from persecution, could no longer boast of Baxters and Bunyans, it is impossible to think without sincere respect of the honourable and laborious lives of such men as Watts, Doddridge, and Lardner, by whom the chances of preferment were voluntarily rejected for conscientious reasons.

I suggest that Leslie Stephen in 1876 was not only more charitable than Christopher Hill in 1967, but also more trustworthy. And in a later lecture we shall see that at least one dissenter whom Stephen named had earned from Dr Johnson not just respect but positive veneration.

I have reached a point where I seem to be defending, not just dissenting Christianity in the early eighteenth century, but eighteenth-century Christianity in general. And I would not go so far as Professor Donald Greene, whose exasperation with this hoary *canard* of the eighteenth century's supposed religious torpor led him a few years ago to suggest in all seriousness that instead of calling this age 'Augustan' we start calling it 'Augustinian'. But we do need to keep open minds, or rather we need to prise open minds (our own) which propaganda over many generations has contrived to close – to close to the possibility that Christian devotion and Christian worship played just as large a part in English life between 1700 and 1740 as in any other forty years of our history. In due course we shall find that nearly all the propaganda to the contrary, whether from the Right or the Left, can be traced to one source in one poet – to William Blake, whose specially perverse and complicated relation to English Dissent I shall touch upon, too sketchily, in a later lecture.

Since I have more than once already struck into a vein of autobiographical reminiscence, I should not like to end this introductory lecture without indulging myself in one further flight, or rather without discharging two further obligations that I am conscious of. In the first place, all the time I was here as an undergraduate there was in the university, had I only known it, one man who could have answered most of my questions, perhaps all of them: Bernard Lord Manning of Jesus College (1892–1941), author of *Essays in Orthodox Dissent* and *The Hymns of Wesley and Watts*. Elegant and searching books, both of them; though, once again, I discovered them only years after I had gone down, and indeed when I was out of England. The right time for me to have discovered them was when I returned from the war with both parts of the Tripos still before me, and by a private arrangement enjoyed through one long summer the hospitality of Cheshunt College, lineal heir of a dissenting academy, renewed as a foundation of the famous evangelical lady, Selina, Countess of Huntingdon. Remembering that Homerton College was also originally a dissenting academy, I cannot help but think that Cambridge – traditionally the Puritan and Cromwellian university – is, for the investigation I propose, not just an appropriate place, but the one right place. And accordingly I am very grateful to Trinity College – not the most Cromwellian nor the most puritanical of houses – for the chance to give these lectures in the place where they may get the most sympathetic, if not the most indulgent, hearing.

Old Dissent, 1700–1740

I WANT TO begin by reading a poem. And since I shall rather seldom in these lectures be able to do this, let us enjoy together while we may the *presence* of poetry, as distinct from more or less impertinent prattle about it. The poem is called 'Man frail, and God eternal', and it will be familiar to most of you, though probably not under that title.

I

O God, our help in ages past,
　Our hope for years to come,
Our shelter from the stormy blast,
　And our eternal home.

II

Under the shadow of thy throne
　Thy saints have dwelt secure;
Sufficient is thine arm alone,
　And our defence is sure.

III

Before the hills in order stood,
　Or earth receiv'd her frame,
From everlasting thou art God,
　To endless years the same.

IV

Thy word commands our flesh to dust,
　'Return, ye sons of men':
All nations rose from earth at first,
　And turn to earth again.

V

A thousand ages in thy sight
   Are like an evening gone;
Short as the watch that ends the night
   Before the rising sun.

VI

The busy tribes of flesh and blood,
   With all their lives and cares,
Are carry'd downwards by thy flood,
   And lost in following years.

VII

Time like an ever-rolling stream
   Bears all its sons away;
They fly forgotten as a dream
   Dies at the opening day.

VIII

Like flowering fields the nations stand
   Pleas'd with the morning light;
The flowers beneath the mower's hand
   Lie withering ere 'tis night.

IX

Our God, our help in ages past,
   Our hope for years to come,
Be thou our guard while troubles last,
   And our eternal home.

Those to whom this poem is not wholly unfamiliar will remember it as sung rather than spoken; and in the second place will remember it in parts and not as a whole. And this establishes two things about it: first, that it is a *lyric* poem, in the strictest pristine sense of 'lyric', and second, that in so far as it has been transmitted to us, the transmission has been oral, not through print. For it is characteristic of orally transmitted poetry that some parts of poems 'drop out', and in fact some of the stanzas I have just read are so habitually 'dropped out' that they may well be said no longer to belong in the poem – in the poem, that is, as it has been smoothed and moulded in the course of oral transmission through one English generation after another. And it is *that* poem – the poem as it has 'come down' to us, not the poem as originally com-

posed and printed – that I am chiefly concerned with. It is wholly
to the point to remark that the poem is for most intents and purposes anonymous, in the sense that not one in a hundred of those
who partly remember the poem will be able to name its author.

What I am describing is a very ancient kind of poem, perhaps the
most ancient kind known to us – from other cultures as well as our
own. What we have here, it seems, is a lay, '*le chant de la tribu*', a
kind of poem that pre-dates not just the age of print but the age
of script, a kind of poem from before writing was invented.

The existence of this kind of poem has been known for a long
time, but it is only quite lately that our knowledge of it has come
to be – for many of us – a worry and a reproach. Most of us who
study literature have lately come to be uneasy, from time to time,
about the extent to which the literature we study is the product
not of 'the tribe' but of a self-enclosed *élite* or priestly caste
within the tribe. We have become ever more frequently agitated
by our awareness that most of what we study and value as 'literature' is just not known, and never has been known, to the mass of
the English nation, or English-speakers across the world. Our discomfort about this, in extreme cases our feelings of guilt about it,
can be allayed by attending to poems like 'O God, our help in
ages past' – a poem that is known to English-speakers far outside
the ranks of any highly educated minority as well as outside any
Christian church; a poem, indeed, that has attained the ultimate
classic status of being known to, and sometimes quoted by, people
who know not what it is, nor who it is, that they quote. Poetry
like this, which has sunk down so far into the common anonymous stock of our linguistic inheritance, can best allay whatever
populist misgivings we have – and most of us have some – about
devoting ourselves, so much of the time, to products of 'high' or
'minority' culture. Accordingly we need not be surprised if
poems like this one are happily seized upon, and attentively
studied, amongst us.

In such a case, I say, we need not be surprised. But what *must*
be our surprise when we discover that the case is quite otherwise?
That even as we bend our energies more than ever before to the
ramifying traditions of the Child ballads, to the recovery and print-

21

ing of anonymous broadsides and street-ballads, of threshers' songs and weavers' songs and children's songs to the skipping-rope (not to speak of barrow-boy poets and Merseyside poets and country-rock poets *à la* Bob Dylan), the attention we pay to a poem like 'O God, our help in ages past' is precisely what it was fifty years ago – which is to say, no attention at all, unless we happen to be either hymnologists or else (less probably) historians of the Nonconformist churches! The reasons we may find for this – mere bad faith, mere sloth, incurious inertia – are true so far as they go; but there are other more specific, historically conditioned, reasons – and these may emerge in due course. For the moment it seems we must say that if 'O God, our help in ages past' represents a very ancient kind of poem, that kind is a great deal too ancient for our self-applaudingly 'modern' criticism to be able to deal with it.

We think of this poem as a hymn. And that sounds right, for 'hymn' is indeed the traditionally appropriate title for one sub-category of the sort of tribal lyric that we seem to have to do with. More precisely, however, our poem is not a hymn but a *psalm*. In fact it is specifically and deliberately a version of one of the Psalms of David, or rather of the first six verses of that psalm, Ps. 90, of which the first six verses in the King James Bible are as follows:

Lord, thou hast been our dwelling place in all generations.

Before the mountains were brought forth, or ever thou hadst formed the earth and the world, even from everlasting to everlasting, thou art God.

Thou turnest man to destruction; and sayest, Return, ye children of men.

For a thousand years in thy sight are but as yesterday when it is past, and as a watch in the night.

Thou carriest them away as with a flood; they are as a sleep: in the morning they are like grass which groweth up.

In the morning it flourisheth, and groweth up; in the evening it is cut down, and withereth.

Need it be said that just such dependence on a sacred or canonical text, and in consequence just such total disregard for 'originality' or 'self-expression', is entirely typical of the poet of the tribal lay? Nevertheless it is clear that our poet has intended more than a metrical translation of the verses of Scripture, such as had been effected for the Psalms by John Calvin himself, by Clément Marot at Calvin's insistence, and in England by Sternhold and Hopkins as well as (memorably) by Philip Sidney and his sister and their collaborators on the Sidney Psalter. Our poet is working in that Calvinist tradition but at the same time transforming it, administering to it a shock which in fact provoked many guardians of that tradition to rise up in arms against him. What he gives us is a psalm, not translated, but paraphrased and modernized, and yet in no sense 'freely adapted', but modernized according to a very strict method. He said himself of these compositions of his that they were 'The Psalms of David Imitated in the Language of the New Testament'. And what this means in effect, schematically, is that every time the ancient Hebrew poet looks back ('Lord, thou hast been our dwelling place in all generations'), our English poet looks back with him, but then immediately looks forward; thus, 'O God, our help in ages past', but then, immediately, 'Our hope for years to come'. Original, he had no wish to be; but independent, a radical innovator, he certainly was. As one of his few modern admirers remarks: 'He worked alone. No pope, bishop, college or committee asked him to undertake his task.' His achievement, she says, is 'a shocking example of Protestant individualism'.

Yet, all this is of no account at all if, when we hear or read or sing 'O God, our help in ages past', it strikes us as merely *dull*. And this may well be the case; for we've already found reasons why current critical precepts, and the reading habits they inculcate, should be ill-adapted to seeing anything responsible or sensitive or distinguished in verses like:

> A thousand ages in thy sight
>   Are like an evening gone;
> Short as the watch that ends the night
>   Before the rising sun.

or: Time like an ever-rolling stream
>   Bears all its sons away;
> They fly forgotten as a dream
>   Dies at the opening day.

23

About such matters there can be no argument – at least in this sense, that no one should allow himself to be browbeaten into pretending that what he registers as 'dull' somehow isn't. All that a lecturer can do is to avow quite sincerely that 'dull' isn't how such verses register for him now, though it's true that once they did; to quote from his author to show that dullness was one risk the author foresaw yet decided to take; and finally to offer what he has found for his own part to be an instructive comparison. This I now proceed to. . . .

In the first place Isaac Watts (for he, of course, is the poet we are dealing with), speaking of such compositions as this one, declared:

> In many of these composures, I have just permitted my verse to rise above a flat and indolent style; yet I hope it is everywhere supported above the just contempt of the critics: though I am sensible that I have often subdued it below their esteem; because I would neither indulge any bold metaphors, nor admit of hard words, nor tempt the ignorant worshipper to sing without his understanding.

and in 'A Short Essay toward the Improvement of Psalmody', he made the same point more vehemently: 'It was hard to restrain my verse always within the bounds of my design; it was hard to sink every line to the level of a whole congregation, and yet to keep it above contempt.' This was a poet who, if he practised what Pope and the Scriblerus Club called 'the art of sinking', did so deliberately, after counting the cost, his eyes open to the risk he was running. His endeavour may be thought to be perverse; it was not at all events mere blundering (and if the question be put whether he was capable of any style more elevated, more exuberant and audacious – well yes, there are poems of his that prove that he was).

As for the comparison, it shall be with a poet of genius, Christopher Smart, whose paraphrases of the Psalms, on precisely the same principles, came almost exactly half a century after Watts's. Smart's version of Psalm 90 as a whole should be examined. His stanzas which correspond to the two quatrains lately quoted are these:

24

For years thy creatures, as they flee,
Are all responsible to thee,
    The present as the past;
Ev'n thousands in thy perfect sight
Are as the watch of yester-night
    When their account is cast.

Thou bidst them off into the deep
Of vast eternity to sleep
    And in their peace remain;
While others like the grass succeed,
For their determin'd goal to speed,
    Nor e'er revolve again.

Does Smart turn to profit the elbow-room that he gets from two extra lines in each stanza? It seems to me quite evident that he does not, that the extra lines, and rhymes, betray him into laxity and vapidity.

Well, but (it may be said) we ask of a poetic style – of a style in any art, and indeed of a style of life – that it possess more than negative virtues. It is a weighty point, and one indeed that takes us at once to the heart of the Calvinist aesthetic. For that is what we are now concerned with. And in the first place a Calvinist aesthetic exists: 'In nothing perhaps has Calvin been more misjudged than in the view that he lacked an aesthetic sense. . . .' It was after all John Calvin who clothed Protestant worship with the sensuous grace, and necessarily the aesthetic ambiguity, of song; and who that has attended worship in a French Calvinist church can deny that – over and above whatever religious experience he may or may not have had – he has had an aesthetic experience, and of a peculiarly intense kind? From the architecture, from church furnishings, from the congregational music, from the Geneva gown of the pastor himself, everything breathes *simplicity, sobriety*, and *measure* – which are precisely the qualities that Calvinist aesthetics demands of the art-object. Just here, in fact, is where negative virtues become positive ones. And this is true not just of Calvinist art but of all art, not just of Calvinist ethics but of all ethics. The aesthetic *and* the moral perceptions have, built into them and near to the heart of them, the perception of licence, of abandonment, of superfluity, foreseen, even

25

invited, and yet in the end denied, fended off. Art *is* measure, *is* exclusion; is therefore simplicity (hard-earned), is sobriety, tense with all the extravagances that it has been tempted by and has denied itself. I appeal to you, and to your experience, whether in making art or in responding to it: Isn't this the way it is? And so, even if we admit for the sake of argument that Calvinism denies sensuous pleasure, we encounter time and again the question, when faced with a Calvinistic occasion: Do we have here a denial of sensuous pleasure, or do we not rather have sensuous pleasure deployed with an unusually frugal, and therefore exquisite, fastidiousness? It is peculiarly of the nature of Puritan art to pose just this question, though that is by no means the account of it that is usually given.

The French critic Brunetière had in mind something different, though related, when he maintained that Calvin's *Institutes* constitute the first book in French of which one might say that it is 'classic': 'It is equally so', he says, 'by reason of the dignity of the plan, and the manner in which the conception of the whole determines the nature and choice of details.' It is important here to take the particular and precise force of the term *classique* in French usage; and Brunetière gives a succinct definition of it in the passage just quoted. In this sense of 'classic' or 'classical' – the subordination of detail to 'the conception of the whole' – Pope is not often classical, and is not so to just the extent that he is, as Dr Leavis showed us, in 'the line of wit'. But classical in this sense is just what, for good or ill, we can call the poet who protested: 'It was hard to restrain my verse always within the bounds of my design. . . .' 'O God, our help in ages past' is in this sharp, Calvinist, non-English sense, 'classical', as are very few poems by Pope, and also incidentally few hymns by Charles Wesley. In fact I suggest that, just as there is a necessary and compelling and often noted connection between Methodistical Evangelicalism and Romanticism, so between Calvinism and 'classicism' there is a connection no less binding. 'Simplicity, sobriety, and measure' – do the words not speak for themselves?

If this should seem paradoxical, the paradox is not of my making. And I should be very sorry to have it thought that this is special pleading. I suggest in all earnestness that the common cause which the English dissenters felt with the Huguenots gave some of them a more direct access to the culture which produced *Athalie*, than Pope could or did get from reading Boileau or Voiture; for after all the Roman Church produces its own puritans, and Racine's *Athalie*, so far as it is Jansenist, is itself puritan art. Unless we disabuse ourselves of certain stereotyped oppositions in our thinking, we shall lose track of the dissenting thread in our culture, even at this early stage. The first such slack assumption that we need to be rid of looks like a ghost of Matthew Arnold's distinction between the Hellenic and the Hebraic emphases in our inheritance. It is the assumption that the more 'classical' a culture is or aspires to be, the less sympathy it will feel with the Hebrew Scriptures, and vice versa. We need to remember that Racine wrote *Athalie* as well as *Phèdre*; that Dryden wrote *The Hind and the Panther* as well as *Macflecknoe*; and that Isaac Watts is as authentic a voice of Augustan England as is Alexander Pope. A second false assumption is likely to be even more obstructive, if only because it is particularly rife at the present day, and is promoted by the false friends of Dissent rather than by its enemies. It can be symbolized by the latest and now current biography of Cromwell, which has the (as I find it) embarrassing title, *God's Englishman*. There is abroad among us an unformulated assumption that Dissent is in some special ways more 'English' than the Church of England is – and this in contexts where 'English' means, more or less defiantly, 'insular'. However it may be in the twentieth century, or may have been in the seventeenth, English Dissent in the eighteenth century was not insular in the least. The full cultural consequences of the influx of Huguenots into England, after the revocation of the Edict of Nantes, has I think never been assessed, nor indeed much studied. But in any case a strong and sturdy 'French connection' can be traced among dissenting leaders from before the seventeenth century is out. More surprisingly, the connection is not only with French Protestantism, still less with the lunatic fringe of that Protestantism, the Camisard 'French prophets' who irrupted upon England in 1709–10 and ultimately spawned, by way of the English prophetess Anne Lee, the Shaker communities in America. Watts and Wesley and Cowper, even the Evangelical poet Henry Kirke White, were respectfully and eagerly aware of 'surprising conversions' within French Roman Catholicism. And Isaac Watts drew upon the Counter Reformation more generally, notably upon the Latin poems of 'the Christian Horace', the Polish Jesuit, Matthew Casimire Sarbiewski (1595–1640). In short, English Dissent does not offer an insular alternative to European culture, a way of 'keeping out', but rather a way of 'going in' on special, and specially rewarding, terms.

In any case, the notion of a Calvinist classicism gives us a vantage-point from which there open up, and stretch away, vistas which may be dizzying but are also (to speak for myself) exciting and very tempting. I must resist the temptation to explore any of them except one. Can I be serious when I offer Isaac Watts as a poet of the tribal lay, a true analogue in Augustan England of David, the bard and warrior king of ancient Israel? Calling Watts to mind, undersized and sickly, demure and grave and domesticated in Hanoverian London, the notion seems ludicrous. And yet I do suggest it. The dissenters for whom he wrote conceived themselves to be, very exactly, 'a tribe', a chosen people just as ancient Israelites were chosen, in tension with their neighbours just as ancient Israel was. Watts shared their conviction, and articulated it for them once and for all, magnificently:

> The Church the Garden of Christ
>
> We are a Garden wall'd around,
> Chosen and made peculiar Ground;
> A little Spot inclos'd by Grace
> Out of the World's wide Wilderness.
>
> Like Trees of Myrrh and Spice we stand,
> Planted by God the Father's Hand;
> And all his Springs in Sion flow,
> To make the young Plantation grow.
>
> Awake, O heavenly Wind, and come,
> Blow on this garden of Perfume;
> Spirit Divine, descend and breathe
> A gracious Gale on Plants beneath.

Make our best Spices flow abroad
To entertain our Saviour-God:
And faith, and Love, and Joy appear,
And every Grace be active here.

Let my Beloved come, and taste
His pleasant Fruits at his own Feast.
I come, my Spouse, I come, he crys,
With Love and Pleasure in his Eyes.

Our Lord into his Garden comes,
Well pleas'd to smell our poor Perfumes,
And calls us to a Feast divine,
Sweeter than Honey, Milk, or Wine.

Eat of the Tree of Life, my Friends,
The Blessings that my Father sends;
Your Taste shall all my Dainties prove,
And drink abundance of my Love.

Jesus, we will frequent thy Board,
And sing the Bounties of our Lord:
But the rich Food on which we live
Demands more Praise than Tongues can give.

There are good examples here of what Watts meant by 'sinking' his style. 'The young Plantation' for instance has little to do with afforestation, but a lot to do with Plymouth Plantation or the Plantation of Ulster – a pungently topical allusion, historically resonant, which might have been elaborated into something ingenious and striking, which instead is subdued to the tenor of the rest. And another example is the way in which 'spirit' and 'gale' in adjacent lines vivify each other by evoking their common element, 'breath'. But it is more important to recognize the strategy and structure of the whole occasion: how the ancient icon and figure of the *hortus conclusus*, the garden enclosed, is startlingly renovated by being applied to religious Dissent. For the 'We' of the first line – 'We are a Garden wall'd around' – is not mankind as a whole, not the whole body of Christians, not even Protestant mankind, but specifically *dissenting* mankind. For what sense would it make to describe the Church of England as 'A little Spot . . . Out of the World's wide Wilderness'? How could this be said of a Church whose head is the reigning. monarch, whose bishops sit as Lords Spiritual in Parliament? The Established Church is the *national* Church; that is what 'establishment' means – it is by maintaining the strenuous fiction that the Church and the nation are conterminous that Anglicans claim and attempt to sanctify or spiritualize the entire secular order. But 'tribe' implies something more intense and intimate than that, a community much more immediately in tension with its potentially hostile neighbours. And Watts's poem articulates that tribal sentiment, just as the royal psalmist articulated it for Israel. Moreover, hymns like this, and perhaps this very hymn, were composed and sung *from manuscript*, week by week through 1694 and 1695, in the dissenting chapel at Southampton to which the youthful Watts had returned from his dissenting academy in the much more sumptuous though still sober milieu of Stoke Newington. (Hence arises the charming tradition that one of the loveliest of them – 'There is a Land of pure Delight' – was prompted by the view of the Isle of Wight across Southampton Water.) Watts was there in the congregation, hearing his hymns sung at sight by his neighbours, most of whom, no doubt, he knew and could name. Can we conceive of a more tribal situation, or of a relation more immediate and intimate between a poet and his public? And this happened at the very height of what we are taught to call 'the age of print', that sad interregnum in the history of poetry from which – we are asked to believe – a Yevtushenko or an Allen Ginsberg or Leonard Cohen has come to save us, by reading his poems through massed microphones and thus (if you please!) reviving poetry as an oral art.

This poem is a hymn, not a psalm. But it is related as closely as the psalm was, to a passage of Scripture – to verses from the Song of Solomon:

> A garden inclosed is my sister, my spouse; a spring shut up, a fountain sealed. . . .
> Spikenard and saffron; calamus and cinnamon, with all trees of frankincense; myrrh and aloes, with all the chief spices;
> A fountain of gardens, a well of living waters, and streams from Lebanon. . . .

I am come into my garden, my sister, my spouse: I have gathered my myrrh with my spice: I have eaten my honeycomb with my honey: I have drunk my wine with my milk: eat, O friends; drink, yea, drink abundantly, O beloved.

And the Song of Songs or (more properly, since it is not one song but many) the Book of Canticles is, we all know, the most erotic item in the Scriptures and one of the most intensely and unashamedly erotic pieces of literature that we know of. How comical, we snigger, that our Puritan forebears should not have noticed that! But *of course* they noticed it, and relished it. If they allegorized it into a nuptial mysticism which made Christ the bridegroom and the Church his bride, they knew perfectly well that allegory can work only if the literal sense is coherent and compelling on its own account. Listen to one of them:

The doctrine of *union* between Christ and his church is of a nature so *copious*, that no one metaphor can *properly* represent it; therefore in the scriptures we meet with *various* similitudes, tending to illustrate the important subject. Christ is frequently compared to a *foundation*, on which his people are built; but that conveying only the idea of support, therefore he is compared to a *root*, by which the idea of *influence* is likewise illustrated. But though *branches* are influenced, and rendered fruitful, in consequence of conveyed nourishment, yet Christian *activity* is not thereby properly represented: to supply this defect, Christ and his people are farther illustrated by the union subsisting between *head* and *members*. But though the idea of *activity* is thereby conveyed, there is still a material defect, for the relation between these is quite *involuntary*. Had it been otherwise, the *head* might possibly have chosen better *feet*, or better *hands*; and had *they* been the subject of distinct volition, they would probably have chosen to have been in union with a better *head*: therefore to supply the deficiency of the above simile, and to include the idea of *mutual choice* and *social endearments*, Christ and his church are compared to *husband* and *wife*. If then we are in such near and close connection with the blessed Jesus, as the Scriptures assert, and, by so many significant similitudes, illustrate his own people to be, let us frequently think of, and bless God for, that *sovereign* and *inseparable* love which constituted the relation. It is all of God, as is acknowledged by that sweet singer in our British Israel, the late Dr. Watts, who of the Father's love and choice thus speaks:

31

Christ be my first elect, he said,
Then chose our souls in Christ our Head;
Nor shall our souls be thence remov'd,
Till he forgets his first belov'd.

This passage, from Robert Hall the elder's *Help to Zion's Travellers* (1781), is an invaluable example of how carefully, with how much sophistication (literary as well as theological), devout Christians of the eighteenth century read Watts's poetry.

Alas, it couldn't last. Haven't Puritans always had a hang-up about sex? (Vague and vulgar language; but these are vague and vulgar notions.) Well, no, it appears that they haven't. But already by 1736 Watts was printing an apology: 'Solomon's Song was much more in use amongst preachers and writers of divinity when these poems were written than it is now.' His friend and follower Doddridge took the hint, and among Doddridge's 363 scriptural hymns, published in the 1750s, not one is derived from the Song of Songs. The emergence of the hang-up, it seems, can be dated quite precisely; and sure enough, *NED* gives 1746 for the first appearance of both 'pruriency' and 'prurient' in their modern senses. After that everyone gets more and more flustered whenever erotic and devotional experience are found close together. John Wesley in a sermon asked about Watts's hymns: 'Are they not too full of expressions which strongly savour of "knowing Christ after the flesh"? Yea, and in a more gross manner, than anything which was ever before published in the English tongue? What pity is it, that those coarse expressions should appear in many truly spiritual hymns!' And Robert Southey in 1837 is close to panic:

> Pure as was the mind of Dr Watts – and its purity was equal to the lucid clearnness of his style – he has in many of these pieces made so bold a use of the sensible imagery proper to amatory verse, that while the unspiritual reader is apt to linger, if not finally to rest, in the mere external sense, there is no small danger, at least in these times, lest the more pious and refined should experience a feeling bordering on disgust.

Whose minds were the more prurient and agitated: Watts's and the Baptist Hall's, or Wesley's and Southey's, both of them High

Church Anglicans? 'Puritanical', it seems, may or may not be right for describing repressed sexuality – it rather looks as if it isn't right – but certainly it is something that crops up in Church at least as often as in Chapel.

While we are about it, we may as well look at some things that have been said about Watts up to our own day. Here is Leslie Stephen in 1876:

> The name of Watts, associated with certain hymns still dear to infancy, has contracted a faint flavour of the ludicrous, though other poems of greater pretensions are still preserved in the lower strata of literature. The hymns, indeed, of Watts, Doddridge, and the Wesleys, whatever their literary merit, have been popular enough to show that they are not inadequate expressions of a strong religious sentiment. It is said that for many years 50,000 copies of Watts' 'Psalms and Hymns' were annually printed: and if there be any truth in the commonplace about songs and laws, Watts' influence must have been greater than that of many legislators, and, indeed, many more distinguished writers. But such an influence is too intangible in its nature to be easily measured.

And that is all we hear from Stephen about Watts's hymns, or Watts's poetry generally! In one who, as Noel Annan says, pioneered, if not 'the sociology of literature', at least the consistent relating of literary to social history, that 'influence . . . too intangible . . . to be easily measured' is surely a very cavalier way of dismissing the phenomenon of Watts's popularity through nearly two hundred years – with English-speakers, moreover, many of whom knew no other English poetry at all. However, we are in no position to jeer at Stephen; for we, too, a century after him, have no way of dealing with such phenomena, no method by which to translate the quantitative facts of so many copies sold and printed year after year, into the qualitative consideration of how they conditioned the sensibility of the English-speaking peoples. What we can and should do, however, is to confess and insist – as Leslie Stephen does not – just what a vast lacuna this reveals in our pretensions to chart cultural history, and diagnose cultural health, on the evidence of printed literature. There is quite clearly *prima facie* quantitative evidence for supposing that Watts's *Hymns and Psalms* ('Watts Entire', as it came to be called) has been more influential than any of the works of its century that we think of as most popular – more than Johnson's *Dictionary*, more than *Robinson Crusoe* or *Gulliver's Travels*, more even than *The Seasons* or 'Ossian'; and so far are we from taking this into account, that the work in question gets either no notice at all or only marginal notice in histories of our literature!

I am not prepared nor competent to rectify this state of affairs; my concern is to probe a little behind Stephen's lordly or flurried parenthesis: 'Whatever their literary merit'. I am trying to show that their literary merit is very great, and hence that, whatever the extent of their influence, it may well have been an influence for the good, a *civilizing* influence. (And if I had time, incidentally, I would have liked to show this for Philip Doddridge, though Watts was a genius whereas Doddridge was only an exceptionally intelligent and honourable and civilized man.)

What Stephen said of Watts – that his name 'has contracted a faint flavour of the ludicrous' because of its association with 'certain hymns still dear to infancy' – is still true today. At least I can find no other explanation when, as late as 1960, a historian of Dissent declares: 'the greatest imaginative literature of Puritanism is to be found in Watts's hymns', but then goes on – inexcusably, I think – to say that this treasure can be found only 'with perseverance in thrusting through the doggerel and bathos'. This image of Watts is potent among us because Watts's name has become attached to just one of his books: his *Divine and Moral Songs for Children* (1720). And Lewis Carroll's lethal because good-humoured and hilarious parodies have conditioned us so that we cannot read with a straight face such rhymes as 'Let dogs delight to bark and bite', or 'How doth the little busy bee Improve each shining hour', or ' 'Tis the voice of the Sluggard: I heard him complain, "You have waked me too soon! I must slumber again!"' ' Not all of these poems by Watts are indefensible. But a defence of them would have to start by placing them in a tradition that runs from Bunyan's *A Book for Boys and Girls: or Country Rhymes for Children* (1686), and takes in the Wesleys' *Hymns and Prayers for Children* (1746), Christopher Smart's *Hymns for the Amusement of Children* (1770), and Mrs

Barbauld's *Hymns in Prose for Children* (1782), to culminate in Blake's *Songs of Innocence* (1790). The development is, as Professor Holloway has shown, from songs *to* or *about* innocence to songs *of* innocence. And in this department of poetry Blake so consummately crowns and transcends all his predecessors, that only by a very strenuous exertion of the historical imagination can we get sympathetic access to the climate of feeling about children which Blake's beautiful poems rule out of court. Such an exertion is possible but I do not attempt nor invite it here; and so the case that I want to make for Watts does not rest in any way on the poems he wrote for children. It should be said, however, that William Blake and Lewis Carroll are redoubtable assailants for any poetic reputation to have to contend with; and what should give us pause is that both Blake and Dodgson thought Watts worth spending their ammunition on, as did Emily Dickinson also.

Between the last two authorities that I have cited came A. E. Housman, in *The Name and Nature of Poetry* (1933), quoting four lines of Watts and declaring: 'That simple verse, bad rhyme and all, is poetry beyond Pope.' As I have declared upon another occasion, this is a great deal worse than useless. Pope is one of the greatest poets in our language, and incomparably the greatest poet of England during Watts's lifetime. Because earlier I have suggested that in one crucial and valid sense Watts's poetry is more classical than Pope's – for in how many poems by Pope do we register the whole as greater than the sum of its parts? – I must make it plain that in no way do I contend for Watts's poetry as superior to Pope's (which would be absurd), nor yet as representing an alternative tradition to his. That would be sectarian indeed! (And it's a trap that sectarian commentators have fallen into.) No! Housman is *exactly* wrong: so far from Watts representing an artless tradition rivalling the artfulness of Pope, what we must see in him is a similar artfulness, though less magisterial, in the service of a quite different artistic end.

And who was the man who wrote these poems that I ask you to admire? Was he *all* poet, or all poet-plus-preacher? By no means! But to establish what Watts stood for, what he signifies and

35

represents, over and above whatever one thinks of his poetry – for this we go to another authority, whose testimony redeems the otherwise shabby story of how the memory of Watts has been preserved amongst us. We go – and I think we might have guessed it – to that most magnanimous of Anglicans, Samuel Johnson. Johnson's estimate of Watts is one of the things I shall take up in my next lecture.

Dissent and the Wesleyans,
1740–1800

AS WE HAVE seen, it is hard to find anyone with a good word to say for the dissenters of the early eighteenth century. Even their fellow-sectaries, in the nineteenth and twentieth centuries, customarily appeal over their heads to their seventeenth-century predecessors. A curious instance of this is the blue-stocking historian Lucy Aikin in 1828, writing across the Atlantic to her fellow-Unitarian, William Ellery Channing:

> As for . . . the Calvinistic dissenters, they had the misfortune of living in one of those middle states between direct persecution and perfect religious liberty, which sours the temper by continual petty vexations, without affording scope for great efforts or great sacrifices – which drives men to find a perverse pleasure in hating and being hated, and to seek indemnification for the contempt of the world in a double portion of spiritual pride and self-importance. 'We can prove ourselves saints', 'being Christ's little flock everywhere spoken against', is the plea put into the mouth of this set by Green, a poet, who was born and bred among them.

Surprisingly, after this contemptuous dismissal of the eighteenth-century dissenters, Lucy Aikin in her very next paragraph pays tribute to the dissenting leader Doddridge, recording how 'my kindred the Jennings, the Belshams, my excellent grandfather Aikin, and his friend and tutor Doddridge, had began to break forth out of the chains and darkness of Calvinism, and their manners softened with their system'. But more immediately to our purpose is her specifying, as the spokesman of 'this set', 'Green, a poet'. This is Mr Matthew Green of the Customs

House, whose most sustained performance, *The Spleen*, is one of those delightful but not very consequential poems that are continually being re-discovered, but never by enough readers to save them permanently from obscurity. For my generation the rediscovery was effected by F. R. Leavis in some well-considered and valuable pages of his *Revaluation*. That was in 1936, and over the years since, unless I am mistaken, oblivion has claimed Matthew Green once again. But as Lucy Aikin may remind us, Green *stands for* something; his poem articulates a particular moment in the spiritual and intellectual history of one kind of Englishman – a moment which otherwise in our poetry goes unrecorded. It's on these grounds – which were not Leavis's – that we may pluck him back from oblivion once more, and for as long as anyone is interested.

To say that Green was a dissenter is true, but misleading. He seems to have been in fact a lapsed Quaker – which is a very special kind of dissenter, special at any time but particularly so in 1737, the year of Green's death, when *The Spleen* was published; for George Fox, the farouche and irreconcilable founder of the Society of Friends, had died as recently as 1691, and the process by which, over no more than two generations, the English Quaker transformed himself from that stereotype into becoming the banker and iron-master of the Industrial Revolution, represents an adaptation so extreme and so precipitate that it must give pause even to someone who believes that 'accommodation' (as I have ventured to call it) was the historically necessary and in itself not ignoble duty of Dissent in this period. Accommodation, yes; but at this rate? And on this scale? One thinks the better of those like Matthew Green who could not change so far so fast.

Horace Walpole said of *The Spleen*: 'It has the wit of Butler with the ease of Prior without imitating either.' And the judgment is less facile than it may seem: Butler's *Hudibras*, pillorying once and for all the Old Dissenters and their pretence to 'the inner light', is consistently the presence behind Green's poem, not just as a formal and stylistic mark that Green must steer by, but as an ideological pressure that he must acknowledge and give way before. Hence, for instance, the dissenters of his time, or else of his childhood, unmistakably and excellently pinned down:

> Nor they so pure and so precise,
> Immaculate as their white of eyes,
> Who for the spirit hug the spleen,
> Phylactered throughout their mien;
> Who their ill-tasted home-brewed prayer
> To the state's mellow forms prefer;
> Who doctrines, as infectious, fear,
> Which are not steeped in vinegar,
> And samples of heart-chested grace
> Expose in show-glass of the face. . . .

The neat, terse gibes strike home; and yet they are predictable, out of common stock. The figure being assailed is after all a stereotype, a cardboard cut-out. Such knowledgeable and spiteful apostasies from Dissent were common in Matthew Green's lifetime; Samuel Wesley the elder is another example out of many. It is permissible to feel that an attempt like Watts's, to change Dissent from inside, was a more honourable and forthright endeavour.

Certainly, we may infer, it seemed so to Dr Johnson, who said of Watts: 'Such he was as every Christian Church would rejoice to have adopted'; who specified Watts's *cultural* achievement by saying:

> He was one of the first authors that taught the dissenters to court attention by the graces of language. Whatever they had among them before, whether of learning or acuteness, was commonly obscured and blunted by coarseness and inelegance of style. He shewed them, that zeal and purity might be expressed and enforced by polished diction.

Johnson it was, moreover, who apologized for a long quotation from Gibbons's memoir of Watts, by saying: 'If this quotation has appeared long, let it be considered that it comprises an account of six-and-thirty years, and those the years of Dr. Watts.' Johnson it was who concluded his account of Watts by saying: 'happy will be that reader whose mind is disposed by his verses or his prose, to imitate him in all but his non-conformity, to copy his benevolence to man, and his reverence to God'. And it was Johnson who, when the name of Matthew Green was missing from the list of poets whom he was to introduce, made no demur; but who, when Watts's name was missing, insisted that it be included – as he is careful to tell us himself, at the start of his 'Life of Watts'. Johnson's 'Life of Watts' is nearer to hagiography than any other of his *Lives of the English Poets*; and if the significance of thus honouring a dissenter is lost upon us, it impressed and puzzled readers nearer to Johnson's time, as we see for instance from Hazlitt's *Conversations with Northcote*.

As regards poetic style, to compare Green with Watts means questioning whether 'conceited' *wit*, however submerged and subdued – as we can find it in Green but not, except in his apprenticeship, in Watts – can be taken in respect of the eighteenth century, as by and large it can be taken when we deal with the seventeenth, as the measure of imaginative seriousness. *The Spleen* itself supplies evidence that, for good or ill, wit-writing was by 1737 restricted to those parts of a composition that were relatively capricious and irresponsible; for at line 717 Green prepares for his exordium by re-addressing his addressee, Cuthbert Jackson, in the person of 'Memmius'. This signals a shift to a graver tone than the inventive banter which has preceded it; and the diction henceforth is nearer to the plain style of Watts than to Marvell:

> In one, no object of our sight,
> Immutable and infinite,
> Who can't be cruel or unjust,
> Calm and resigned, I fix my trust;
> To him my past and present state
> I owe, and must my future fate.
> A stranger into life I'm come,
> Dying may be our going home,
> Transported here by angry Fate,
> The convicts of a prior state;
> Hence I no curious thoughts bestow
> On matters I can never know.

This passage, which some readers will think the most moving and the most seriously intended in the poem, is almost entirely free of wit. On the other hand it is a profession of faith so hedged about with saving clauses – consider only that 'Dying *may be* our going home' – that it can hardly be called 'Christian' at all. Indeed, could it not be subscribed to by any number of nineteenth or twentieth-century agnostics? And isn't this the reason why, when – rarely, as by Leavis – we are directed to *The Spleen*, we are able to respond to it so warmly? In any case it is all very well to say (what is true) that in Green's more vivacious passages we see the urbanity and ease of Andrew Marvell's octosyllabic couplets persisting into the eighteenth century; but we need to count the cost – that in order to reproduce this alert suavity Green permits himself a flippant or weary impudence about the tents of Christian belief such as Marvell eighty years before neither could nor would have allowed himself.

Nevertheless *The Spleen* is invaluable, indeed irreplaceable, for giving a lively and highly intelligent account of the state of mind and feelings in which a dissenter of the 1730s might either conform to the Establishment or slide out of Christian belief altogether. There is no denying that in the 1720s and 1730s such defections and apostasies were very common. The numbers of the faithful were falling precipitately; and historians for whom as it were the box-office returns are the ultimate test have no difficulty showing that dissenting leaders like Watts and Doddridge quite manifestly in their generation *failed*. This was the reasoning of Elie Halévy when in 1906 he addressed himself to 'The Birth of Methodism in England'. Of the Methodist evangelists Wesley and Whitefield, Halévy says that 'they reanimated, as a side effect of their influence, the other Dissenting sects, which were seemingly dying of old age'. More sweepingly Halévy asserts: 'after fifty years (1688–1738) of professing religious skepticism England had her Puritan revival, and the date can be established firmly; it was in 1739 that the crisis occurred.' One does not lightly disagree with an authority like Halévy, and yet on this point he seems to be quite simply *wrong*. Moreover he backs it up with special pleading. Thus, when Doddridge in his *Free Thoughts* asked that the minister be 'an evangelical, an experimental, a plain & an affectionate preacher', he was not, as Halévy supposes, an exception that proves some quite opposite rule. Nor do the dissenting sermons of the time bear out Halévy when he

41

declares: 'The Dissenting ministers should have been able to assume the leadership of the Protestant opinion; they were its chosen chiefs. But betraying the confidence of their followers, they preached a doctrine more and more like that of Aristotle or Cicero, instead of Christianity according to Saint Paul.' How is it possible to recognize in this description the most famous and influential dissenting minister of the time, the Isaac Watts who wrote that hell-fire sermon in plunging sapphics, 'The Day of Judgment'?

> Hopeless immortals! how they scream and shiver
> While devils push them to the pit wide-yawning
> Hideous and gloomy, to receive them headlong
>   Down to the centre!

Is *that* the doctrine of Aristotle or Cicero? We are likely to find it very unaccommodating indeed! And it requires a considerable exertion of the historical imagination to recognize, in the face of such a document, that 'accommodation' (to secular enlightenment and civility) was nevertheless Watts's and Doddridge's steady endeavour – as Johnson realized.

Halévy is not the first to be so dazzled by the massive and heroic figure of John Wesley as not to realize how there could be, and was, resistance to his evangelizing on scrupulous and considered grounds. 'When the Methodists started to preach', he assures us too confidently, 'they were well received by the great majority of Dissenters':

> Was not the religion they preached a revival of Puritanism? But they ran up against the distrust and hatred of the ministers, too enlightened and reasonable to enjoy the doctrine and method of the Awakening. And that is why those ministers were not themselves capable of bringing forth an Awakening; and why the Awakening could not come from the Dissenting Churches.

Even if all this were true, might we not conclude that the congregation failed their ministers, rather than the other way round? That by and large the ministers were too far ahead of their flocks, pursuing a cultural 'accommodation' that their congregations were not ready for? This would avoid having to use 'enlightened' and 'reasonable' as words of opprobrium, when applied to such men as Doddridge or Watts or Edmund Calamy; and it would be in the spirit of Johnson's tribute to Watts.

How some dissenting ministers responded to the Wesleyan challenge may appear from a piece of admirably vigorous mid-century prose:

> I will take this occasion with great freedom to tell you my opinion of those people who are called Methodists. I have carefully inquired after them; was willing to think well of them; loth to censure them or hear others do so. And I think still there are serious people deluded by them. But after a candid attention to them, their proceedings appear not to be wise and good. Their devotion is unseasonable, irregular and injudicious. Their sermons are low and loose and not at all like what they seem to assume. Their spirits appear to me to be turbulent, unruly and censorious. They practise upon weak men and poor people. They call them up to pray and sing when they should be in their business or their beds. They disturb the peace and order of families. What they pretend above their neighbours, appears to me mere enthusiasm. Their people are rather slothful, mopish and dejected or pragmatical, than sober, considerate, judicious, exemplary and regular Christians. And I have no expectation but that Methodism, like other enthusiasm, will promote infidelity and turn out to the damage of religion and the souls of men. Though I judge not their hearts, views and motives, which are secret things that belong to God, yet I thought it needful very lately to warn my hearers of these people's errors and advise them to avoid them.

This is one of the remonstrances that Philip Doddridge endured in 1743 when he had allowed George Whitefield to preach from his pulpit. Others came from Watts, from John Guyse, and from a trustee of the Coward Trust thinly veiling a threat to withhold Trust funds from Doddridge's Academy; and if this makes it seem that Doddridge was more 'liberal' than his fellow ministers, the point is that on this flank he could afford to be – his distrust of 'enthusiasm' was well established, and it was on his other flank that he was vulnerable, where he joined hands with the more or less Arian circles that we have seen Lucy Aikin connect him with. He represented firm and consistent opposition to Methodism from within Dissent – an attitude that we can find for instance in his friend and editor Job Orton up to the latter's death in 1783. And indeed, though it could be said in 1806 that 'the Independents have gone over in a body to the Methodists', there was, as we shall see, opposition from Old Dissent to the Methodist New Dissent until far into the succeeding century.

To return to Elie Halévy. . . . His theories about the *birth* of Methodism have been overshadowed by his much more startling and influential argument as to its consequences: an argument advanced in his classic work of 1912, *England in 1815*, though in fact it was already firmly formulated by 1906. The argument is that 'England was spared the revolution toward which the contradictions in her polity and economy might otherwise have led her, through the stabilizing influence of evangelical religion, particularly of Methodism'; in other words, that the potentially revolutionary energies of the unprivileged English were syphoned off by the Wesleys and Whitefield into activities not political at all, but religious. This hypothesis in fact did not originate with Halévy; on the contrary, the bare bones of it are to be found not just in several British and French nineteenth-century historians but in Robert Southey in the first decade of the nineteenth century and indeed in the Methodists themselves as they defended themselves against the punitive measures against them proposed in 1811 by Sidmouth, the Home Secretary. Moreover, 'Halévy, like Weber, was suspicious of all efforts to understand history as the product of a single cause, and he saw religion as capable of altering what appeared to be the otherwise almost "inevitable" tendency of the internal contradictions (as both Ricardo and Marx understood them) of the new industrialism to produce Revolution'. Marxist historians are thus uncomfortable about Halévy's hypothesis, with a discomfort that is compounded by the fact that the hypothesis is rather plainly the product of a speculative and indeed literary intelligence in Halévy, rather than of 'scientific' research. In these circumstances it is remarkable that the hypothesis still stands, and that claims, by Marxists and others, to have overthrown it turn out on examination to be quibbles and qualifications not affecting the central contention, which is that the revolution which ought to have been 'inevitable' was in fact evaded. Accordingly, when a Marxist historian takes over Halévy's thesis, he does so with a specially bitter feeling of mortification.

This is compounded by the historically incontrovertible fact that Wesleyan Methodism springs out of the Moravian movement of Count Zinzendorf, which itself is plainly related to the egalitarian and enthusiastic 'Ranters' of Cromwell's time – a body, or an obscure congeries of bodies, long enshrined in English Marxist mythology as heroic pioneers and precursors. How with equanimity concede that this tradition which should have been, and once was, proto-revolutionary should, in the Wesleys' lifetime and for long after, have produced a movement that was consistently, and at times splenetically, High Tory? Certainly, in the nineteenth century, radicals and trade-union organizers were often Methodists; and in our time some Methodist historians have made much of this. But it is incontestable that radicals like Hazlitt and Leigh Hunt and Cobbett saw Methodism in their day, with reason, as on the contrary a bulwark of the *status quo*.

There is a yet further complication, in the fact that when John Wesley finally broke with the Moravians it was because of the insistent yet devious and grotesque eroticism which characterized their hymns certainly, and perhaps other aspects of their worship also. No one who has looked at the Moravian hymn book of the 1740s will want to deny that Wesley acted with good taste and good judgment in deciding that this would never do. Yet this circumstance is awkward for the Marxist historian when he wants to establish that in Wesleyan hymns 'Love' is private and airless, whereas it ought to be 'social'. Our historian levels the charge none the less:

> the cult of 'Love' was brought to a point of poise between affirmations of a 'social religion' and the pathological aberrations of frustrated social and sexual impulses. On the one hand, genuine compassion for 'harlots, and publicans, and thieves': on the other hand, morbid preoccupations with sin and with the sinner's confessional. On one hand, real remorse for real wrong-doing: on the other, luxuriating refinements of introspective guilt. On one hand, the genuine fellowship of some early Methodist societies: on the other, social energies denied outlet in public life which were released in sanctified emotional

onanism. . . .

> . . . Here was a cult of 'Love' which feared love's effective expression, either as sexual love or in any social form which might irritate relations with Authority. Its authentic language of devotion was that of sexual sublimation streaked through with masochism: the 'bleeding love', the wounded side, the blood of the Lamb. . . .

We notice how far this twentieth-century authority agrees with the eighteenth-century dissenter, in finding the Methodists 'slothful, mopish and dejected'. But he has in his sights something quite specific, a body of achieved literature, Charles Wesley's hymns. And this being so, the disciplines of the social historian will serve no longer. All sorts of further considerations now arise – notably the tradition in devotional literature of images of the Lamb and Bleeding Heart, at least from the counter-reformation on; and the traditional use of the erotic analogy over the same period. For instance, is Watts's Calvinism of 1710 to be allotted the same socio-historical significance as the Wesley's Arminianism of the 1750s, because of Watts's unabashed use of the eroticism of the Song of Songs?

And not only sexual organs like the lips are to be ruled out, but liver and lights also; for we are told:

> after the Wesleys broke with the Moravian brethren, the language of their hymns . . . had become a public scandal. In the hymns of John and Charles Wesley overt sexual imagery was consciously repressed, and gave way to imagery of the womb and the bowels:
>
> > Come, O my guilty brethren, come,
> >   Groaning beneath your load of sin!
> > His bleeding heart shall make you room,
> >   His open side shall take you in. . . .

Not all readers will be sure that they find in these indifferent verses either bowels or womb. But if we do find them, what follows? Are all bodily functions and organs too gross to serve as analogies and imagery in poetry, or in devotional poetry? Whoever is being 'puritanical' in this confrontation, it seems not to be Charles Wesley.

However, what our historian can't stand the sight of is blood. And there is blood all over the place in the Wesleyan hymns 'as if the underground traditions of Mithraic blood-sacrifice which troubled the early Christian Church suddenly gushed up in the language of 18th century Methodist hymnody'. 'The union with Christ's love', Edward Thompson decides (for he it is that I am quoting), 'unites the feelings of self-mortification, the yearning for the oblivion of the womb, and tormented sexual desire', for 'sacrificial, masochistic, and erotic language all find a common nexus in the same blood-symbolism'. And so to the indignant peroration:

> It is difficult to conceive of a more essential disorganisation of human life, a pollution of the sources of spontaneity bound to reflect itself in every aspect of personality. Since joy was associated with sin and guilt, and pain (Christ's wounds) with goodness and love, so every impulse became twisted into the reverse, and it became natural to suppose that man or child only found grace in God's eyes when performing painful, laborious or self-denying tasks. To labour and to sorrow was to find pleasure, and masochism was 'Love'. It is inconceivable that men could actually *live* like this; but many Methodists did their best.

But this is beyond a joke. A very strenuous protest is surely called for – not on behalf of Methodism, nor on behalf of Christianity (though it is Christianity as such, not just Methodism, that is the target of this sort of rant), but on behalf of poetry; for if poets are to be judged in this way, by scraps of verses torn from their context in poems and their larger contexts in iconographic and literary tradition, with a flurry of words like 'masochistic' that have no place in either literary or social history, which of all our poets will 'scape whipping?

Yet the fault lies with our literary historians, for what I remarked of the hymns and psalms of Watts – that we look in vain through our literary scholarship for any considered assessment of their intrinsic virtues and their historical significance – is hardly less scandalously true of the more than 6,000 hymns composed by Charles Wesley. Where the literary historians have so shamefully failed to do their duty, one can hardly blame the social historian for rushing in. I would not be misunderstood. The text of the Wesley hymns has been reliably established, and this was no light undertaking in respect of such a bulky corpus; there has been valuable examination of Wesley's metres; and a great deal has been done by way of identifying sources and analogues and allusions. The *editorial* challenge has been met. In particular, like every one else who has poked his nose into this field, I must pay tribute to Henry Bett's admirable *The Hymns of Methodism*. But it is precisely the 'field' that must be questioned; Charles Wesley's poetry is thought to be a very special field indeed, something *sui generis* or at most to be compared with a few hymns by other hands. One looks for a long time before finding any attempt to place Charles Wesley, or Isaac Watts either, in relation to the more secular poetry of their times – in relation to Pope, or Thomson, or Gray or Goldsmith. One consequence is that the eighteenth century is thought to have produced little *lyric* poetry, whereas the eighteenth-century lyric is to be found in the hymn books just as surely as seventeenth-century lyric is in George Herbert's *Temple*. The dependence of line after line of Wesley on the precedent of Matthew Prior has been duly noted, but no one has explored the significance, stylistically and historically, of this surprising connection with the suave and frequently improper author of 'Henry and Emma'. Methodism is a sub-culture as Old Dissent is a sub-culture; and the tribal warmth of such a sub-culture, of what Edmund Burke called 'our own little platoon', is so comforting and agreeable that there is no more incentive from within its ranks to relate the sub-culture to the national culture, than there is on the part of the Establishment to acknowledge what manoeuvres the little platoons have been engaged in.

Yet John Wesley, in striking contrast to his fellow evangelist Whitefield, was at great pains not to let his followers cut themselves off from the culture of the national society as a whole, particularly not from the *literary* culture. He used his *Arminian Magazine* for many purposes; but among them was keeping in currency George Herbert and Prior and other writers he valued. He printed there, to the scandal of some of his readers, Prior's 'Henry and Emma', which Johnson the High Churchman found improper. In his late *Thoughts on the Character and Writings of Mr. Prior*, as in such a stray document as a letter of 1764 to the

Reverend Mr Furley, Wesley was a master of very acute and un-prejudiced practical criticism. Moreover his successful battle through his lifetime to keep Methodism within the Established Church is something that tells the same story: Wesley did not want to found a sect, and he distrusted the tribal, the sectarian temper in culture. On this point his brother the poet was even more determined: Charles jeered and mocked when John began ordaining his own preachers. For the brothers were very different, though they co-operated loyally. It was Charles, the poet, for instance, who governed his sex life better, who made a successful marriage and reared a happy family; and it was Charles's house-hold that rang night and morning with music, some of it highly sophisticated.

One literary scholar has lately broken through the sectarian ring that otherwise still walls off Charles Wesley's poetry from English poetry generally. This is Martha Winburn England, in a volume on which ten years ago she collaborated with John Sparrow for the New York Public Library. To this book, entitled *Hymns Unbidden*, Miss England contributes a series of excep-tionally erudite and perceptive papers comparing Wesley with his contemporary William Blake. Blake certainly knew Wesley's work: his autograph, dated 1790, appears in a copy of Wesley's *Hymns for the Nation, in 1782.* Written by Charles Wesley when the defeat of British forces by the American colonists was clearly inevitable, *Hymns for the Nation* sees 'America as Sodom, her leaders as murderers and fanatics, the Continental Congress as like Lucifer in its rage for power and its blind fury of insurrec-tion', and the American Loyalists as 'martyrs, persecuted by usurpers and betrayed by weak leadership'. Blake, of course, saw Washington and his colleagues quite differently, 'not as Albion's enemies but as allies of that visionary spirit of liberated energy as it existed in Britain'. But what matters is not that Wesley and Blake drew opposite conclusions, but that they addressed themselves to the same problem, and in the same spirit; for, as Ms England puts it: 'What *Hymns for the Nation* has in common with Blake is belligerence, exuberance, excess.' And this is, throughout their careers, the common ground between these two poets:

Lecture 3

'Wesley and Blake are comparable in their arrogance, vulgarity, and excess. These traits of enthusiasm entered into all their poetic successes and can be seen with greatest clarity in their poetic failures.' But they shared also a common intention: 'Their poetry is prophetic and evangelical, the messages are intensely personal and aimed at reformation of the social order. They meant to bring about an inner change, in the heart, the imagination, and hoped that social changes would come about as a result.'

It is against this background, of the temperamental affinity between the two men and their common dedication to a prophetic role, that the differences between them stand out most sharply. And their political differences are among the least important. In the first place, 'Wesley looked upon himself as transmitting a received dogma', whereas Blake 'claimed no connection with any existing orthodoxy'. If Blake can be called Christian at all (which may well be doubted) 'his Christianity has no institutional aspect at all. All his life, he neglected those ''means of grace'' to which the Wesleys refer most often'. He seems never to have taken communion nor to have attended any services other than his own christening and wedding. Second, 'the authority of academic standards of excellence had no part in Blake's aesthetic. He thanked God he was never sent to school.' Wesley on the other hand was associated with scholarship all his life. Hence, third, 'Blake professed antagonism to empirical philosophy, experimental science, and the lower and higher criticism of the Bible that were an important product of the Enlightenment', whereas Wesley accepted these ideas early in his life, and wrote his hymns in the light of them. Then again, in Ms England's words:

> An obvious difference is Wesley's acknowledged obligation to clarity. He wrote in three traditions that demanded it. The Augustan aesthetic demanded it, and he added to that demand his own emphasis on the didactic nature of his writings and the nature of the audience he addressed. . . . None of these pressures operated directly upon Blake. He would not accede to demands for a certain sort of 'clarity', for it involved the writer in those generalizations which seemed to him a blurring of true clarity.

But over and above all these differences, there is one that goes deeper: where Wesley believes in paradox, Blake believes in dialectic. And anyone who attends with proper seriousness to the matters which preoccupied these two nobly dedicated men must, on this crucial issue, side with one of them against the other. R. H. Tawney, who was no worse a theologian and no worse a Christian for being also a historian and a Socialist, remarked:

> There is a distinctively Christian way of life. . . . This way of life is not, as appears often to be supposed, identical with what is called 'goodness'; for . . . Christianity is a religion for sinners. It rests on a peculiar – and superficially, at any rate, a highly improbable – view of the nature of the universe. It implies the acceptance of a scale of spiritual values which no rationalisation can make appear other than extremely paradoxical.

'Extremely paradoxical' – just so:

> What though my shrinking flesh complain,
>   And murmur to contend so long,
> I rise superior to my pain,
>   When I am weak then I am strong,
> And when my all of strength shall fail,
> I shall with the God-Man prevail.
>
> My strength is gone, my nature dies,
>   I sink beneath thy weighty hand,
> Faint to revive, and fall to rise;
>   I fall, and yet by faith I stand,
> I stand, and will not let thee go,
> Till I thy name, thy nature, know.

In these lines, where our social historian would no doubt discover 'masochism', the central paradox of a god who is also man breeds other paradoxes, as that weakness is strength, and falling is rising – as it was for the God-Man who triumphed by being crucified. Such paradoxes are at the heart of Wesley's writing, as of any writing in the centrally Christian tradition; and time and again the laborious clarity of Wesley's verse takes on rhetorical splendour and intensity when paradox is concentrated into its appropriate rhetorical figure, oxymoron. Blake is not so much incapable of this, as profoundly averse to it. This emerges, for instance, when Martha Winburn England compares him with Charles Wesley as regards another of the central Christian paradoxes – that Law is Love: 'Wesley believed law and love were one, paradoxically related in time, but eternally one. Blake . . . saw no sweetness in commandment or statute, no love in any discipline imposed from without'. Paradox is what Blake cannot readily live with, though his 'Tyger' is certainly a splendid exception. His famously *dialectical* way of thought solves and evades paradox by separating it out as it were on a plane surface: love ('Innocence') *leads to* law ('Experience'), as law then *leads to* love (through Revolution). Paradox is multivocal; Blake has to break it down into narrative sequence, into the univocal. Though Blake is commonly thought of – and in part rightly – as an enemy of rationalism, in this defining feature of his thought he is a rationalist all through.

Thus, Blake's relation to English Dissent is tortuous and very far from clear. G. E. Bentley has presented evidence, inconclusive but suggestive, that Blake's father about 1769 joined a Baptist church; and this, if true, would clarify the all but unanimous contention of the early biographers that Blake's parents were dissenters, though no one says of what kind. The question is academic, however, for it has come to seem more and more likely – ever since A. L. Morton's *The Everlasting Gospel* of 1958 – that the Dissent which *effectively* influenced Blake was that of the antinomian and heretical sects, the Ranters and Muggletonians, who (as is now clear) survived in clandestine fashion among the artisans and petty tradesmen of London, from their origins in the Cromwellian Commonwealth until Blake's lifetime and after. These sectaries are now attracting much devoted and admiring attention. But it is not denied by their most fervent admirers that what they express is socio-political resentment and aspiration thinly cloaked in religious terminology; and that, as specifically *religious* insights, their ideas are beneath contempt. Thus none of the research currently being pursued into the Muggletonians and others can seriously qualify the impression that in Blake, as – so I shall suggest – in D. H. Lawrence a century later, we have a case of an imaginative genius born into a stratum of religious experience too shallow to sustain him.

John Holloway has shown invaluably how many of Blake's

'Songs of Innocence and of Experience' are cast in the metrical, the rhetorical and stanzaic forms of Watts's and Doddridge's hymns; and indeed the connection with Watts was noticed as early as 1806. But it must be emphasized that the theological content that is poured into these moulds is such as Watts and Doddridge would have been appalled by, and would have denounced as un-Christian.

One may think William Blake a great poet, and an exceptionally engaging person, and still regard with alarm, as a very ominous symptom, the veneration which nowadays is so freely accorded him; for what we see, I suggest, as the aristocratic Anglicanism of George Herbert modulates into the Old Dissent of Richard Baxter and Watts and Doddridge, and then is overtaken by the evangelizing of the Moravians and Wesleyans – is a test case, historically recorded, of what happens when a body of difficult but momentous truths is taken 'to the people'. To those who draw from this record the sanguine conclusion that in the process nothing, or nothing important, was lost – I have nothing to say. For those who believe that something was lost along the way, it is very difficult to determine just where, in the process, the simplifications and intensifications became 'too much' – so as to damage just those truths that were to be simplified and intensified. To speak for myself, I am much persuaded by those who point to the excesses of the Wesleyan meetings – the fallings about, the paroxysms, the 'speaking with tongues', and the preachers' perfervid and foolish rhetoric that provoked such manifestations – as clear symptoms of religious sentiment perverted, and doctrine coarsened out of recognition. But then I encounter the wonderful figure of John Wesley himself, who regretted these grotesque distortions and diagnosed them (as in his comments on the Flemish prodigy, Antoinette Bourignan), who none the less tolerated them as a price that had to be paid – Wesley, whose level-headedness and fastidious though heartfelt taste is manifest on nearly every page of his that has come down to us. What does seem to me certain is that, by the time and to the extent that the process works itself out in Blake, the game is not worth the candle, the price asked (and paid by Blake) is exorbitant. Blake is lamed by this historical process, not – except in the delusory short run – sustained by it; he is not a hero of the democratizing of Scripture, but a martyr to it.

Dissent and the Evangelicals, 1800–1850

HORTON DAVIES, in one of his admirable volumes on *Worship and Theology in England*, has shown that George Whitefield was a much better theologian than is commonly supposed. But on the other hand he has to censure, in Whitefield, his 'philippics against book-learning and his pietistical and puritanical assumption that pleasure itself was a pursuit unworthy of a Christian'. Davies points out – what cannot indeed be emphasized too often – that 'Such a philistinism was unthinkable to Wesley, for whom reason, after Scripture, was an avenue of the knowledge of God'. And 'philistinism' seems not too harsh a word for Whitefield, the preacher who declared: 'Our common learning, so much cried up, makes men only so many accomplished fools.' However, when Horton Davies describes this attitude as 'puritanical', he is – while not wrong, for common usage regrettably supports him – certainly misleading, for as we have seen, such dissenters as Watts and Doddridge stand on this issue squarely with Wesley, not with Whitefield – so much so indeed that they have to be defended from the opposite imputation, of being 'cold reasoners'. And the same holds true, perhaps more surprisingly, of dissenters of an earlier, more rugged, kind – of a Richard Baxter or a Matthew Henry, whose *Commentaries* I remember on the bookshelves of my Baptist grandfather. And yet, if we think a little, this should not surprise us; for in Old and New England alike the dissenting ministers were typically martyrs to erudition, as witness the monumental works that they composed. Matthew Henry's *Commentaries* of 1710 certainly constitute such a monument; and it is interesting to see what Henry makes of a Scriptural text that might seem to give colour to an attitude like Whitefield's, the verse from Ecclesiastes which declares: 'For in much wisdom is much grief; and he that increaseth knowledge increaseth sorrow.' Matthew Henry in his comments on this passage interposes a special note, which runs:

> it becomes great men to be studious, and delight themselves most in intellectual pleasures. Where God gives great advantages of getting knowledge, he expects improvements accordingly. It is happy with a people, when their princes and noblemen study to excel others as much in wisdom and useful knowledge, as they do in honour and estate; and they may do that service to the commonwealth of learning, by applying themselves to the studies that are proper for them, which meaner persons cannot do.

Did the old Puritan have in mind perhaps such a contemporary as the great Robert Boyle? We cannot be sure; but we *can* be sure that in his mind 'the commonwealth of learning' was not limited to studies like theology and church history, nor yet to those as supplemented by such useful disciplines as accountancy and mechanics. For he is himself glad to call upon the elegant speculations of Sir William Temple when the course of his commentaries has brought him to those books of Scripture which he recognizes without fuss as 'poetical'.

The point, it will be realized, is an important one. Distrust of intellect, of rational discourse and free enquiry, and distrust of the arts – these attitudes, though they can be found among Puritans (for philistines can crop up anywhere), seem not to be characteristic of seventeenth-century Puritanism, and certainly do not characterize its lineal descendant, eighteenth-century Dissent. And yet common usage, as we all know and have just seen, asserts the contrary. How can this be? I will answer brusquely, trusting you to gather from this series of lectures as a whole the evidence on which my answer is grounded: first, the Establishment (in its strict sense, as the Church of England) has in every generation, including our own, disseminated the *canard* that Dissent is of its nature philistine; and, second, in the nineteenth century, Dissent co-operated, by becoming as philistine as the

Church had always said it was. In this, English Dissent betrayed its own tradition; and the melancholy story of that betrayal is what I now embark upon.

But the first impetus towards the philistinism of nineteenth-century Dissent came not from Dissent but from inside the Anglican Establishment; and the label to be tied on it is not 'puritanical' but rather 'Evangelical'. This too, however, is a word that must be used with caution. Evangelical with a small 'e' is what every man of God must hope to be, a description in which every one of them should take pride. Even Evangelicalism with a capital 'e' is not altogether right if we take it, as is commonly done, to comprehend Wesleyanism. But the charge lies heavily indeed against the other two branches of what the historian Horton Davies distinguishes as Evangelicalism: that is to say, the Calvinistic Methodism of George Whitefield and the Countess of Huntingdon's Connexion, and second, the closely associated Anglican Evangelicals who 'attained the dimensions of a party in the first three decades of the nineteenth century'. These last have never enjoyed a good press from imaginative writers, nor do they deserve one now from any one concerned with the history of our culture in any sense of that word. Indeed, since the publication of Brown's *Fathers of the Victorians* (1961), the one cultural achievement which it seemed could be laid to their credit, the practical humanitarianism of Wilberforce and his allies, has been so blown upon that it has disappeared, and shows up on the debit side; for Ford shows convincingly that an Evangelical publicist like the famous Hannah More was acting thoroughly in the spirit of Wilberforce himself, when she inculcated the most rigid Tory sentiments in the poor people whom she reached with her tracts. And the Toryism in question is not that of the hearty eighteenth-century squirearchy, nor yet that which was to come with Disraeli, but the openly repressive Toryism of Pitt and Sidmouth and Castlereagh during the French Wars and the post-war wretchedness that exploded in the breaking of the weavers at Peterloo. Politically, indeed, the Evangelicals under Wilberforce not only supported Pitt through thick and thin so long as he worked for the one cause they had set their hearts on, the abolition of the slave trade, but it can be argued that this strategy of bending all energies towards one definable objective – after the slaves were emancipated it became, significantly, foreign missions – had the perhaps intended effect of stifling all protests at more pervasive and inflammable injustices, nearer home.

However that may be, of the philistinism of the Evangelicals there can be no doubt. The monstrous legacy of it is still with us, as ecclesiastical eyesores: the churches that they built, mostly either sham Gothic or Greek Revival. The Roman Catholic architect Pugin, in his pungent *Contrasts* of 1836, spoke of these Anglican neo-Gothic churches as 'Protestant monstrosities in the garb of Catholic antiquity'; and Ruskin, the other great champion of a truly *inward* Gothic revival, declared in *Modern Painters:*

> The group calling themselves Evangelicals ought no longer to render their religion an offence to men of the world by associating it only with the most vulgar forms of art. It is not necessary that they should admit either music or painting into religious service; but if they admit either, the one or the other, let it not be bad music nor bad painting.

As for the *intellectual* philistinism of the Evangelicals, Leslie Stephen speaks with the authority of direct personal and family experience when he says:

> The history of the Evangelical revival illustrates the limits of religious movements which spring up in the absence of any vigorous rivals without a definite philosophical basis. They flourish for a time because they satisfy a real emotional craving; but they have within them the seeds of decay. A form of faith which has no charms for thinkers ends by repelling from itself even the thinkers who have grown up under its influence. In the second generation the abler disciples revolted against the strict dogmatism of their fathers, and sought for some more liberal form of creed, or some more potent intellectual narcotic. The belief generated in the lower or middle social strata was utterly uncongenial to the higher currents of thought, and, thus confined within narrow limits, ossified into a set of barren theories, never vivified by contact with genuine thought.

How this worked out in practice may appear from a document relatively early in the history of Evangelicalism, a curious passage in Southey's *Life of Henry Kirke White* (1807), where we read

that the friend who converted Kirke White to evangelical principles adduced as proof of his lamentable infidelity his 'having
more than once suggested, that the book of *Isaiah* was an *epic*,
and that of *Job a dramatic*, poem'. Yet as regards the Book of Job
this had been contended for, not only by the famous Robert
Lowth, later Lord Bishop of London, in his epoch-making
Lectures on the Sacred Poetry of the Hebrews (given in 1741 and
published in 1753, to be eagerly studied by Christopher Smart),
but also at the very beginning of the eighteenth century by the
dissenter Matthew Henry. It is plain that, though of course not
all Evangelicals were so callow and provincial as this, none the
less Evangelicalism was in very crucial ways a putting of the
clock back.

Yet it was also very much in tune with the spirit of its times,
for it is plainly in its way a profoundly *romantic* movement, as we
may see from the poetry of this same Kirke White, the Reverend
Charles Simeon's Cambridge prodigy, dead in 1806 at age
twenty-one, a sort of Evangelical Chatterton. Kirke White's
tragic name is the only one that the Evangelicals might claim to
have added to the canon of English poets, though they recruited
as it were posthumously both John Newton and William Cowper,
co-authors of the *Olney Hymns*.

At this period in fact 'puritanism', if by that we mean a distrust
both of open-minded speculation and sensuous pleasure, was to be
found at least as much in the Established Church as among the
dissenters – inevitably so, since it came in the train of the rejuvenated strict Calvinism which Evangelicalism imbibed from Whitefield and Toplady and (it must be said) Cowper, all of them
Anglicans. Nevertheless, it must at once be conceded that even
before the eighteenth century was out, there were Evangelical
dissenters as well as Evangelical Anglicans, and that they were as
philistine as their comrades of the Establishment. The most
damning evidence is once again in architecture and furnishings
for worship. Surrey Chapel, on the south bank of the Thames,
was in being even while John Wesley was alive. It could seat a
congregation of 2,000, and organ recitals were given there
because the chapel possessed a better organ than any London

church. Erik Routley, a historian of Dissent writing for a series called 'English Institutions', says of this development:

> The family has given place here to the massed congregation, and this technique of massed congregations appealed to Dissent in a manner which the Dissenters of the seventeenth century would have found incomprehensible. Preaching gradually developed, in the new large towns, out of the pattern of patient and formal exposition into the pattern of red-hot exhortation and dramatic religious demagogy. . . . To accommodate the great congregations the meeting-houses were often pulled down to make way for large edifices 'in the Gothic style' . . . in their outward architecture eloquent of the ambition and success of Dissent. . . .

and he decides:

> There was, with all the pomp and circumstance of the new-rich nonconformity, a softness at the centre which too often made the new Puritans content with cheap but pretentious buildings, second- and third-rate music, and a sentimentality in popular religion which a realistic twentieth-century generation has justifiably rejected.

If we ask what created that 'softness at the centre' which infects dissenters and Anglicans alike under the stress of the Evangelical Movement, the answer (I submit) is very clear; it was that 'enthusiasm' which accordingly Watts and Doddridge had been so right to distrust and oppose. Dissent came to it relatively late and in many cases reluctantly, but it was in the end destroyed by it (as a cultural force) far more completely than the Established Church where it originated. It could be controlled, barely, so long as John Wesley was alive; after his death it was defenceless before such homegrown hot-gospellers as George Whitefield or Rowland Hill or (I'm afraid we must say) William Blake.

Nevertheless Dissent *did* put up a struggle. There *were*, until well on into the nineteenth century, distinguished dissenters who clear-sightedly tried to hold fast to their inheritance from previous centuries, even as the tides of feeling round them rose and sank. One may even maintain, looking forward to a figure like the late Victorian writer who called himself 'Mark Rutherford', that the Old Dissent of Isaac Watts survives as a slender thread through all the Victorian generations into our own era. But that case can be argued only with large and damaging qualifications, as we shall see. At any rate, the resistance of Dissent to Evangelicalism is a chapter of our cultural history that so far as I can see remains to be written; and though I can't pretend to write it here and now, it is what I shall be concerned with for the rest of this lecture.

The existence of an Evangelical and an anti-Evangelical wing to Dissent at the start of the nineteenth century is neatly graphed in the fortunes of two important magazines. One, the *Evangelical Magazine*, was founded in 1793 as a joint venture of dissenters and Evangelical Churchmen and 'soon became the most widely circulated religious miscellany in England'. It was denounced by the High Churchman Southey in 1808 and again in 1838 for the deplorably wide influence of its Calvinistic philistinism. In 1805 the *Eclectic Review* was similarly started by dissenters and Churchmen jointly, in hopes of pleasing all denominations 'by entering into a compact of neutrality on disputed points of secondary importance'. But the hope was not realized, the Anglicans withdrew their support after a year, and when a new series was started in 1814 the 'compact of neutrality' was explicitly renounced. Thereafter the *Eclectic Review* was maintained successfully for twenty-three years by Josiah Conder, under whom the regular staff included for several years both Robert Hall and John Foster. It was a very different affair from the *Evangelical Magazine*, devoting not more than a quarter of its space to religious topics and – especially admirable – maintaining a department for reviews of foreign literature. Though its standard for poetry was 'still based on eighteenth-century preferences', it declared *Lyrical Ballads* 'one of the boldest and most fortunate adventures in the field of innovation'.

What provoked the Evangelicals to denounce the *Eclectic* was 'Zeal without Innovation', printed by the *Eclectic* in 1810 and written by Robert Hall the Baptist. Hall had at this time left his ministry in Cambridge and was in Leicester where he was to remain until 1826, five years before he died. But it was during his Cambridge ministry, from 1791 to 1804, that Hall achieved fame; and since the Cambridge of Charles Simeon and poor Kirke White was a centre of the Evangelical infection, it is pleasant to reflect that Hall's powerful antidote was being concocted at the same time, not many yards from Simeon's rooms in King's.

Not that Hall was every inch a Cambridge man. In one sense, of course, he couldn't be, since dissenters couldn't be members of the university. But his affection for the place was in any case something short of besotted. His contemporary and biographer, Gregory, recalls him in 1797 or soon after:

> In him all was at the utmost remove from gloom or moroseness. Even the raillery in which he indulged showed his good-nature, and was exceedingly playful; and, notwithstanding the avowed and lamentable impetuosity in argument to which he was prone, nothing, so far as I ever saw, but conceit, ingrafted upon stupidity, provoked his impatience, and called forth a severity which he scarcely knew how to restrain. . . . And such was his prevailing cheerfulness that he seemed to move and breathe in an atmosphere of hilarity, which indeed his countenance always indicated, except when the pain in his back affected his spirits, and caused his imagination to dwell upon the evils of Cambridgeshire scenery.

> This was, in his case, far from a hypothetical grievance. It seriously diminished his happiness at Cambridge, and at length was the main cause of his quitting it. In one of my early interviews with him, before I had been a month at that place, he said to me, 'What do you think of Cambridge, sir?' 'It is a very interesting place'. 'Yes, the place where Bacon, and Barrow, and Newton studied, and where Jeremy Taylor was born, cannot but be *interesting*. But that is not what I mean; what do you say to the scenery, sir?' 'Some of the public buildings are very striking, and the college walks very pleasing; but. . . .' and there I hesitated: he immediately added, 'But there is nothing else to be said. What do you think of the surrounding country, sir? Does it not strike you as very insipid?' 'No, not precisely so'. 'Ay, ay: I had forgotten; you come from a flat country; yet you must love hills; there are no hills here.' I replied, 'Yes, there are; there are Madingley hill, and the Castle hill, and Gogmagog hill'. This amused him exceedingly. . . . '. . . Gogmagog hill is five miles off, and many who go there are puzzled to say whether it is natural or artificial. 'Tis a dismally flat country, sir; dismally flat. Ely is twelve miles distant, but the road from Cambridge thither scarcely deviates twelve inches from the same level; and that's not very interesting. Before I came to Cambridge I had read in the prize poems, and in some other works of fancy, of 'the banks of the Cam', of 'the sweetly flowing stream', and so on; but when I arrived here I was sadly disappointed. When I first saw the river as I passed over King's College Bridge, I could not help

exclaiming, Why the stream is standing still to see people drown themselves! and that, I am sorry to say, is a permanent feeling with me'. I questioned the correctness of this impression, but he immediately rejoined, 'Shocking place for the spirits, sir; I wish you may not find it so; it must be the very focus of suicides . . .'

If such a passage sounds like a smudged carbon-copy of some page from Boswell's *Life of Johnson*, both Gregory and Hall were aware of it. Taxed with the affectation, Hall admitted it:

> Yes, sir: I aped Johnson, and I preached Johnson; and I am afraid with little more of evangelical sentiment than is to be found in his essays: but it was youthful folly, and it was very great folly. I might as well have attempted to dance a hornpipe in the cumbrous costume of Gog and Magog. My puny thoughts could not sustain the load of the words in which I tried to clothe them.

The evangelical sentiment that Hall there regrets his lack of is, of course, very much evangelical with a small 'e', such as Doddridge, too, would have wished to have. As for the Johnsonian manner, it seems to have been one thing that Hall shared with another Cambridge worthy, the once famous eccentric Dr Samuel Parr, greatly influential in his generation though now hardly remembered. Hall and Parr were intimate from 1799 onwards. Three years before, at the trial of John Binns, a Jacobin who had made contact with the naval mutineers at Spithead and the Nore, Parr is said to have helped get Binns acquitted by sitting directly in front of the jury and scowling with disbelief throughout the case for the prosecution, nodding vigorously at points made for the defence; for Parr's Whiggism – he was called 'the Whig Johnson' – was in the 1790s that of Charles James Fox and of the minority in Parliament which consistently opposed the war with France, and Hall at one time agreed with him, as we see from his *Apology for the Freedom of the Press* (1793), provoked by a riot of Cambridge loyalists who had victimized a local liberal, Musgrave, much as a similar mob in Birmingham had earlier victimized the Unitarian Priestley. Both Parr and Hall moved politically to the Right, as revolutionary France became Bonapartist France; and in 1800 a famous sermon on 'Modern Infidelity Considered' brought down upon Hall charges of political apostasy, just as similar swings over the same period brought the same charges against Wordsworth and Southey and Coleridge. What Hall learned from Samuel Parr was thus not political theory, but (apparently) nothing more momentous than the habit of smoking, to which Parr was notoriously addicted. Concerned about this, Gregory gave Hall a pamphlet against smoking by Adam Clarke, to have it returned with the comment: 'Thank you, sir, for Adam Clarke's pamphlet. I can't refute his arguments, and I can't give up smoking.'

All this adds up to a picture very far indeed from whatever stereotype we may have of the dissenting minister of any century, including our own. And the portrait is not uniformly admirable, nor engaging; there are moments at which Hall and Parr alike may strike us as early examples of a type that has cropped up in every English generation to the present day: pint-size Dr Johnsons, Great Chams of the Senior Combination Rooms (or for that matter of dissenting academies), their inconsistencies and quirks lovingly paraded for the benefit of some non-existent Boswell. But this is too harsh; Robert Hall was perhaps not quite a great man, but he was certainly a very remarkable one, and a man of principle. This shows up in the obvious place, which is also the place where we are least likely to look; that's to say, in his theology. For instance, at a time when the sacraments were largely disregarded in all denominations – in St Paul's Cathedral on Easter Day, 1800, there were just six communicants – Hall, in his definition of the meaning of the Lord's Supper, restated the doctrine of the Eucharist in its full and exacting and mythic grandeur. And the significance of this, for those of us concerned with the imaginative arts (whether we are Believers or not), ought to be obvious; for the moment, the point may be gestured at by my admittedly questionable epithet, 'mythic'. And incidentally, if we are surprised to find such sacramental truths affirmed by a dissenter, this I'm afraid proves only our ignorance; for despite their insistence on 'the preaching of the word', dissenters of the seventeenth and eighteenth centuries, contrary to what is supposed, laid very great stress on the sacrament of the Lord's Supper in particular. As regards Hall's theological position in general, it will be remembered that it was his own father who had helped to wean some of the Baptists from an ultra-Calvinist position, and so, although Edwards on the Will was studied by him repeatedly and admiringly, Hall, when asked if he was Arminian or Calvinist, could reply: 'Neither, sir . . .' adding however, 'but I believe I recede farther from Arminianism than from Calvinism.' When he adds further: 'I regard the question more as metaphysical than religious', he is being evangelical with a small 'e'.

All in all, I believe we may think that Hall's Johnsonian pretensions were not all affectation, but testified to a measure of real affinity, for the figure which emerges, even from such scanty impressions as these, is distinctly non-Romantic. It should not surprise us to hear that 'he thought Gray's Elegy the finest thing ever written'. In the *Eclectic Review*, we remember, the magazine that Hall wrote for, 'the standard for poetry was still based on eighteenth-century preferences'.

However this may be, we cannot help but think, with the advantage of hindsight, that it was inevitable the conservative Dissent that Hall stood for should have been swamped before the new century had advanced at all far. Part of the reason for this was a sudden accession to the ranks of Dissent by many new schismatic sects; notably the Primitive Methodists in 1812, the Plymouth Brethren in 1827–30, and the Catholic Apostolic Church in 1835. The Methodists, once John Wesley's hand had been removed and their sectarian status had been acknowledged, were particularly addicted to schism; and the Primitive Methodists were only one of several breakaway Methodist churches, though of particular interest to social historians because of their espousal of the cause of the agricultural labourer. Thus assailed on two flanks – by an Evangelical Establishment, and by these proliferating varieties of New Dissent, Old or Orthodox Dissent could not for long hold by its distinctive emphases, especially since it could not profit by Romanticism, as its more charismatic rivals on both flanks were able to do.

Strictly speaking Old Dissent at this period may be held to comprise only two denominations: the Baptists, and the old Independents who now were calling themselves Congregationalists. (Dissent has its snobberies, and even today it is hard for a Congregationalist not to regard the Methodist as a parvenu.) However, there are at least two other churches which can be thought of as borderline cases between the Old Dissent and the New. These are the Unitarians and the Sandemanians, and I want to consider one representative of each of these.

My Unitarian shall be Elizabeth Gaskell, born and raised a Unitarian and married to a Unitarian minister. In her second novel, *Ruth* (1853), Mrs Gaskell showed great courage, not only by dealing compassionately with the scandalous topic of the un-married mother but, even more outrageously for some readers, by letting her ruined maid's benefactor, a dissenting minister, pass her off as a widow so as to spare her social ostracism. The particular dissenting persuasion of this minister is left unclear, though in fact the original was the Newcastle Unitarian, William Turner. This Unitarian strategy, of consistently presenting themselves as members of Dissent though orthodox Trinitarian Dissent of course disowned them, was first evolved in the 1770s and has done vast damage to Dissent ever since. In any case, the minister who is the hero of *Ruth* is as far as possible from what Mrs Gaskell called in a letter of 1849 'all the cursing evangelicals'. And indeed a Unitarian Evangelical is unthinkable, a sort of *lusus naturae*, for the Unitarians were, and always had been since the days of Joseph Priestley and Richard Price and Mrs Barbauld of the Warrington Academy, an enlightened intellectual minority, particularly strong in those North West Midlands where the Gaskells were in touch with such Unitarian dynasties as the Wedgwoods and later the Darwins. Birmingham was another of their centres. And yet another provincial stronghold of Unitarianism was Norwich, its strength symbolized there by Thomas Ivory's Octagon of 1754–6 – the most elegant meeting-house in England, or perhaps in Europe. From Norwich came Harriet Martineau (1802–76), an even more famous Unitarian bluestocking (and incidentally novelist) than was Mrs Gaskell. It was Harriet's brother James (1805–1900) who was to inspire a Unitarian revival in late Victorian times, for in Elizabeth Gaskell's youth Unitarianism was losing adherents; William Hale White in *The Autobiography of Mark Rutherford* presented it as being spiritually even more sterile than orthodox Dissent, and all the evidence supports him. Meanwhile, as Elizabeth Haldane remarks demurely, 'the sect was small but extraordinarily intellectual and efficient, and if born within it, it was impossible not to gaze at the world from a rather superior angle'. One should set against that Augustine Birrell's testimony that his father, a Liverpool Baptist minister through thirty years, though he admiringly heard both Cardinal Wiseman and Cardinal Manning preach, would have found it unthinkable to enter a Unitarian chapel.

It could be argued, and with justice, that the Unitarians have, in proportion to their numbers and their relatively brief history, made a greater contribution to English culture than all the other dissenting sects put together. Certainly this would be plausible if we proceeded simply by counting heads, enumerating the distinguished individuals who have emerged from among the Unitarians to contribute to the intellectual life of the nation. But, much as we must guard against any sentimentally populist understanding of 'culture', it is undeniable that Unitarians seem in almost every generation to have regarded themselves as an intellectual *élite*, 'gathered' from the world more self-consciously and haughtily than even those other sects which were surest of being 'the elect'. Whereas in some of the other sects – for instance in Congregationalism at certain periods – we find traces of a social *élitism*, this seems never to have been so chillingly exclusive as the intellectual *élite* of the Unitarians. And 'intellectual' can be given another inflection also: the cultural contributions of the Unitarians have been overwhelmingly in speculative thought, in ideas rather than images, arguments rather than fictions, chains of reasoning rather than artifacts. Elizabeth Gaskell is important because she is probably the nearest we can come to finding an exception to this rule. And yet it is generally conceded that even in her case – and one thinks of novels of hers much better than *Ruth* – arguments and ideas, 'causes' and propagandist intentions, lie up too close and manifest below the surface of her stories for us to think of her as a great novelist in the sense in which we are happy to applaud George Eliot or Dickens or Emily Brontë. It is important to get this right. It isn't a matter of setting up cold *head* (the Unitarians) against warm *heart* (the Methodists); that is as unfair to the redoubtably hard-headed Wesley as to the warm-hearted Priestley. None the less, 'rationalist' is certainly what Unitarianism was originally and has remained, with whatever that may imply of imaginative constrictedness and timidity.

I now turn, lastly, to the Sandemanians; and I take as their representative one of the most astonishing geniuses of nineteenth-century England, the scientist (or rather, more properly, the *natural philosopher*) Michael Faraday (1791–1867).

The Sandemanian Church came into being in 1730, founded by an anti-Establishmentarian Scottish Presbyterian minister, John Glas (b. 1695). It was greatly strengthened in 1760 when it was joined by the Inghamites, followers of Benjamin Ingham (1712–72) who, though one of Wesley's earliest associates, broke away and evangelized on his own account, chiefly in the West Riding. The sect takes its name from Robert Sandeman, John Glas's son-in-law (d. 1771), who formulated Glasite doctrine in *Letters on Theron and Aspasia* (Edinburgh, 1757) and *Some Thoughts on Christianity in a Letter to a Friend* (Boston, 1764). William Godwin, the author of *Political Justice* (1793) and of *Caleb Williams* (1794), was brought up as a Sandemanian in Wisbech.

The Sandemanians, though strict in many ways, in others were surprisingly liberal. They did not share, for instance, the traditional dissenting prejudice against the theatre, and Michael Faraday was a theatre-goer. He had no aversion to works of the imagination generally. His wife's niece recalls him in the 1820s:

> My uncle read aloud delightfully. Sometimes he gave us one of Shakespeare's plays or Scott's novels. But of all things I used to like to hear him read 'Childe Harold'; and never shall I forget the way in which he read the description of the storm on Lake Leman. He took great pleasure in Byron, and Coleridge's 'Hymn to Mont Blanc' delighted him. When anything touched his feelings as he read – and it happened not unfrequently – he would show it not only in his voice, but by tears in his eyes also.

The dissenters generally treated Lord Byron tenderly – which may appear less odd when one recalls that Byron is formally and stylistically the most conservative of the Romantic poets. More unexpected is the name of Coleridge; Faraday may have imbibed respect for him from his own early mentor and patron, Humphry Davy. But more surprising still is Faraday's tolerance of novels, for instance of the novels of Scott; for in 1821 Coleridge was still protesting that: 'Walter Scott's novels are chargeable with . . . ministering to the depraved appetite for excitement. . . .' Altogether Faraday's Sandemanian household in the 1820s seems to have been at least as open to the literary culture of that time and earlier as was any establishment household, and a great deal *more* open than Evangelical households.

The demurrer is obvious: wasn't Faraday's Sandemanianism, and indeed his dissenting allegiance generally, merely nominal? The answer is: No. His Victorian biographer is plainly looking through Faraday's own eyes, when he declares:

> The most remarkable event of his life in 1840 was his election as an elder by the Sandemanian Church; he held the office only for three years and a half. During that period when in London he preached on alternate Sundays. This was not entirely a new duty. From the time of his admission into the Church he had been occasionally called upon by the elders to exhort the brethren at the week-day meetings; now, however, it was done regularly. . . .

It is worth pausing here to recall that Faraday was by this time internationally famous and lionized. More to the point, despite the brilliance and profundity of his scientific discoveries, he was not – nor had he ever been – a recluse of the laboratory; on the contrary, he was the interpreter and representative of scientific culture to English society as a whole. In particular, he was a brilliant though scrupulous popularizer of science – principally through his lectures at the Royal Institution which, quite apart from being a crucial source of revenue to that establishment, were highly fashionable and much frequented occasions in the cultural life of early Victorian London. Yet between the accomplished lecturer and the preacher there was a vast gulf:

The reason why his sermons seemed inferior to his lectures is very evident. There was no eloquence. There was not one word said for effect. The overflowing energy and clearness of the lecture-room was replaced by an earnestness of manner, best summed up in the word devoutness. His object seemed to be, to make the most use of the words of Scripture, and to make as little of his own words as he could. Hence a stranger was struck first by the number and rapidity of his references to texts in the Old and New Testaments, and secondly by the devoutness of his manner. These sermons were always extemporary, but they were prepared with great care.

Of the two preaching 'patterns' that Erik Routley cites – on the one hand, 'patient and formal exposition', on the other, 'red-hot exhortation and dramatic religious demagogy' – it is plain which one was favoured by Faraday.

So it should come as no surprise to find him profoundly mistrustful of 'enthusiasm'. This is plain from what he said, as late as 1859, when asked about revivalism:

The Revivals, &c., cannot trouble the Christian who is taught of God (by His Word and the Holy Spirit) to trust in the promise of salvation through the work of Jesus Christ. He finds his guide in the Word of God, and commits the keeping of his soul into the hands of God. He looks for no assurance beyond what the Word can give him, and if his mind is troubled by the cares and fears which may assail him, he can go nowhere but in prayer to the throne of grace and to Scripture. No outward manifestation, as of a revival, &c., can give either *instruction* or *assurance* to him, nor can any outward opposition or trouble *diminish his confidence* in 'Christ crucified, to the Jews a stumbling-block, and to the Greeks foolishness; but to them who are *called*, Christ the power of God and the wisdom of God'. If his attention is called to the *revivals*, it cannot be that he should feel instruction there or assurance there, other than what he finds in the Scriptures, without reference to them; and it seems to me that any power they may have over his mind other than the Scripture has, must be delusion and a snare. That man in his natural state is greatly influenced by his fellow-creatures and the forms of emotion which are amongst them, is doubtless true, even when it concerns what he considers his eternal welfare. How else would the wonderfully varied and superstitious forms of belief have obtained in the world? What carries the Mormons into the desert, surrounded by trouble and the enmity of those around them? What sustains a spiritual dominion like the Papacy, aided by the nations around it, to proclaim the name of Christ whilst it contradicts His Word – refuses it (the record of the Spirit) to the people – and crushes out with all intolerance the simple obedience of the truth? Man's natural mind is a very unstable thing, and most credulous, and the imagination often rules it when reason is thought to be there. Mesmerism has great power over it; so has poetry; so has music; so has the united voice of the multitude; so have many other things: but these things are, so to say, indifferent as respects the *character* of the object they may be used to sustain, and are just as powerful in favour of a bad cause as a good one. Among the contradictory and gross systems of religion, or the numerous and opposed systems of political government, any one of them may be sustained by the use of such agencies as these.

We have already seen that Faraday's apprehension of the profoundly ambiguous effects of poetry upon the imagination does not imply any aversion to poetry, or prejudice against it – quite the contrary. What is notable is his naming as another agency influential on the imagination 'the united voice of the multitude', so averse was Faraday to 'demagogy', and indeed (I think we must say) to mass-democracy. He was in fact strikingly a-political, yet his modern biographer calls him roundly, and not without justice, a Tory.

In conclusion, it is much to the point to ask how Faraday came by the knowledge and the skills which enabled him to realize his promise as a great scientist. It is common knowledge that in the eighteenth century the dissenting academies taught the rudiments of natural science (and sometimes more than the rudiments) as the universities did not; and so it may seem unsurprising that Faraday should, like the chemist Priestley, have come from among the dissenters. But in fact Michael Faraday's origins were too humble for any academic training at all, and he was self-educated. Let a confessedly 'partial portrait', no more than five years old, describe Faraday's education:

Perhaps I should mention that Dr. Isaac Watts, now scarcely remembered, and then as a pompous eighteenth-century hymn-writer, was once the authority on self-improvement, on studying hard, on keeping the mind open and free of prejudice, on learning from experience, and so on. Faraday's earliest publication is a small lecture he gave in his twenties, exclusively based on Watts, about means of learning: from observation, from reading, from conversations with people –

about their own knowledge, about commonly interesting topics, and so on.

This information is supplied more accurately as well as more elegantly by other biographers; I quote this one, Joseph Agassi, for his memorable expression of what Isaac Watts's reputation has become in the second half of the twentieth century. Faraday's textbook in fact was Watts's *Improvement of the Mind*, of which Johnson said: 'Whoever has the care of instructing others, may be charged with deficience in his duty if this book is not recommended.'

I shall draw on Joseph Agassi for one last observation which, though not much less oddly phrased, is in fact more valuable:

> What is real . . . in the last analysis, is the dream, says Jorge-Luis Borges. In Faraday's case it was the dream of the philosophic men and their tranquillity and liberalmindedness that was the most real thing. Deep down, Faraday was the last representative of the Age of Reason and as such the link between the classical and the new Enlightenment. But his religious sectarianism and his political conservatism made him a nineteenth-century man.

Agassi cannot really think that 'religious sectarianism' and 'political conservatism' were unknown in the eighteenth century. Yet by saying hastily what he cannot mean, he betrays suppositions which I suspect knock about in the heads of many of us – for instance, that if there were religious sectaries in our eighteenth century, they cannot ever have been 'politically conservative' (unless, perhaps, they were Wesleyans). On the contrary, of course, the distrust of enthusiasm by a dissenter such as Watts – that 'pompous eighteenth-century hymn-writer' – inevitably made him opposed to whatever was 'democratical'. And so Agassi is not all in the wrong. The link with the Age of Enlightenment *was* there in Faraday; it was precisely his sectarianism that forged the link and made it hold.

Dissent and the Agnostics, 1850–1900

UNLESS WE HAVE a rather exact knowledge of sectarian church history – knowledge that few of us have – we shall misread many Victorian novels. I need not expatiate on this because the case has been made, exhaustively, by Valentine Cunningham in his erudite and disconcerting book, *Everywhere Spoken Against*. I shall briefly consider only one case – that of Bulstrode in George Eliot's *Middlemarch*, particularly as this portrait is related, or has been related by critics, to George Eliot's own religious upbringing. Born to an Anglican household, she seems to have gone first to an Evangelical school run by a Mrs Wallington, and then to the school of the Misses Franklin, daughters of that Francis Franklin who is reputedly the original of Rufus Lyon, a lamentably sentimentalized character in *Felix Holt*. This school is described as 'strongly Calvinistic', on the grounds that the Misses Franklin were Particular Baptists and so, a modern commentator assures us, 'we may presume' that they taught 'Calvinism in its strictest form'. The error here is at least partly the confounding of the Particular Baptists with the Strict and Particular Baptists, followers of William Gadsby (1773–1844) who led a neo-Calvinist reaction within the Baptist Church against what he called 'Fullerism' – that is to say, the middle-of-the-road Calvinism espoused by Robert Hall's contemporary, Andrew Fuller. But in any case the presumption that we are invited to make is unwarranted, for the Particular Baptists 'except for their insistence on Believers' Baptism, are doctrinally and liturgically indistinguishable from the Independents (or Congregationalists)'.

The expressions 'General Baptist' and 'Particular Baptist' are in any case misleading, since in the first place the Particulars seem to have outnumbered the Generals at all times through the periods we're concerned with by at least two to one; and second, it was the Arminian General Baptists who in their practices were more 'radical' and 'primitive'. The Particular Baptists seem to have been no less vulnerable than the Independents to Baxterian and other, even deist or Arian, modifications of their Calvinism. These considerations suggest that Particular Baptist attitudes may not have been at all what George Eliot had in mind when creating Nicolas Bulstrode. Of Bulstrode we are told that before he became the effective master of Middlemarch – as banker, businessman and philanthropist – he had belonged to a dissenting church at Highbury; and our commentator assures us: 'the Church was, significantly, Calvinist'. But in fact the Calvinism of Bulstrode's dissenting background is hardly significant at all, since all of orthodox dissent, except for the General Baptists, claimed to be Calvinist in the mid-nineteenth century as in the mid-eighteenth, and the label could be, and was, pasted on to quite 'liberal' doctrines. Moreover, George Eliot herself explicitly warns us not to see in Bulstrode any cautionary example as to one set of doctrines rather than another. 'This implicit reasoning', she says in chapter 61, speaking of Bulstrode's casuistry, 'is essentially no more peculiar to Evangelical belief than the use of wide phrases for narrow motives is peculiar to Englishmen'. We should do well to take her at her word. This is by no means to deny that George Eliot's sympathies in her fiction could take her beyond the positions she might take up in letters or essays; between her essay on 'Evangelical Teaching: Dr. Cumming' and her sympathetic though detached portrait of the Evangelical clergyman Edgar Tryan in 'Janet's Repentance', there is a wide gap, and one that does her credit. The point to be made rather is that in our literary and social historians alike the term 'Calvinistic' is a catch-all bogey-word, possessing, often enough, no strictly accountable meaning at all.

George Eliot of course 'lost her faith'. And in this she was representative of a substantial body of mid-Victorian intellectuals.

Another who went the same road was Leslie Stephen. More than once already we have drawn upon Stephen's *History of English Thought in the Eighteenth Century*; and this is no more than just, for Stephen's great work of 1876 deserves its classic status. The chapter of most interest to students of literature is the last; and the degree to which the hundred pages of that chapter survive or withstand changes of taste and opinion over a century is truly remarkable. Certainly Stephen's reading of eighteenth-century literature is infinitely less dated than that of his father-in-law, Thackeray, in *The English Humourists of the Eighteenth Century*. Stephen is at his best when he writes of Doddridge's proposals in 1729 for 'reviving the dissenting interest':

> The general spirit of his advice was that the dissenting minister should try to please everybody. His antagonist seems to have hinted at the propriety of a separation between the bigots and the persons of 'generous sentiments'. Doddridge wished the minister to become 'all things to all men'. That was rather too markedly the leading principle of his own life. The eminent dissenter was on friendly terms with the established clergy, and corresponded with bishops; he had relations with Wesley and the Methodists; he was a spiritual adviser of Lyttelton, and of the converted rake Colonel Gardiner; and his academy, once, at any rate, was honoured by the presence of a duke's nephew. Such intimacies, cultivated by the dissenting schoolmaster in a country town, indicated considerable powers of attraction. His life was honourable, independent, and laborious; but we may, perhaps, surmise, without injustice to a good man, that his emotions were rather facile, and that his temptation was to err on the side of complacency. There is a want in his writings of that firmness which is produced by the bracing air of more vigorous times; they show a tendency to flabbiness, and the enthusiasm has but a hollow ring.

This is certainly not the last word on Philip Doddridge; but it is one thoroughly plausible interpretation of the man as we know him through his writings and the record of his life. However, this is conspicuously not true of what Stephen says about Watts:

> In his doctrinal writings there are signs of the diffuse sentimentalism which not infrequently accompanies a feeble constitution. . . . The sermons, however, show something of the old unction. They appeal strongly to the inward witness of the spirit, with a comparative in-

difference to the ordinary evidential argument. Unlike most of his contemporaries, he addresses the heart rather than the intellect; and in his hands Christianity is not emasculated Deism, but a declaration to man of the means, by which God pleases to work a supernatural change in human nature. . . .

Grateful as we must be to Stephen for rebutting in advance the glib generalizations that Halévy was to make about the dissenters' preaching on the eve of the Wesleyan phenomenon, all the same the betraying sentence here is the first: Watts was of 'a feeble constitution'. But so was Leslie Stephen, until he strenuously over-compensated for it by making himself a boat-club hearty when he was Director of Studies at Trinity Hall, and thereafter by assaulting Alpine peaks with the help of the best guides that money could buy. Lord Annan is surely right to relate this to the fact that Stephen's highest compliment is 'manly'. (So it was also for his contemporaries, Pater and Hopkins; we can only guess at the sexual anxiety that this may point to, in the three of them.) 'Manly' was the epithet that Stephen could apply to the Latitudinarian bishop, Samuel Clarke. He could not apply it to Watts; and this is what flusters him.

As for Stephen's inability to do anything at all with Watts's devotional lyrics, his being completely at a loss to categorize or account for them becomes less surprising when, some pages later, he is speaking of the Wesleyan movement, and remarks: 'The want of a sound foundation in philosophy prevented the growth of any elevated theology, and alienated all cultivated thinkers. *One outward symptom of the deficiency is the absence of any literature possessing more than a purely historical interest*.' Not for the first time in this enquiry, the astonished italics are mine. Charles Wesley's hymns, which to this day are sung every Sunday throughout the English-speaking world, in Protestant churches of whatever denomination, are literature of no more than 'purely historical interest'? Yes, indeed. Turn to the index to Stephen's massive two volumes and you will find that Charles Wesley, the poet of Methodism, rates not a single entry. For that matter, Stephen roundly asserted: 'Sacred poetry and religious novels belong to a world of their own' – a world, that is, outside literature proper.

When Stephen gets to the end of the eighteenth century and deals with emergent Evangelicalism, he speaks with more authority, and more acceptably. Yet even here he cannot be trusted implicitly:

The new Puritanism, excluding all the most powerful intellectual elements, was therefore of necessity a faint reflection of the grander Puritanism of the seventeenth century. The morality founded upon it showed the old narrowness without the old intensity. The hatred of the world was too often interpreted into a hatred of all that makes the world beautiful, combined with a hearty appreciation of everything that adds to its material comfort. The tendency which has been the most conspicuous weakness of the creed was the reflection of the tendencies of the English middle classes. Their religious emotions were coloured by the general character of their lives. Protestantism, as it has been developed amongst industrial communities, bears traces of its origin; and though it has produced an heroic type of character, it has always been hostile to the aesthetic development of the race, and to the more delicate forms of religious doctrine.

In that last resounding generalization (which is surely implausible – one thinks, among Stephen's contemporaries, of the undoubtedly puritanical John Ruskin), Stephen is merely parroting a hoary *canard* of the Establishment. Before long a Bishop of Chester was to quote approvingly an authority who declared: 'No doubt the Puritans were often narrow and boorish; they belonged mainly to the middle and lower classes, which in England have never been distinguished by the intellectual graces'; and Froude, writing of Bunyan in the 'English Men of Letters' series, was to present him as 'poet-apostle of the English middle-classes imperfectly educated like himself'.

In particular, of course, Stephen in 1876 was echoing a commination pronounced upon Dissent seven years before in *Culture and Anarchy*. When Matthew Arnold in that book denounced the narrow-mindedness of Dissent in his day, he was in his turn echoing what his father had said thirty years before. 'My fondness for Greek and German literature', wrote Thomas Arnold, 'has made me very keenly alive to the mental defects of the Dissenters as a body; the characteristic faults of the English mind – narrowness of view, and a want of learning and a sound critical

77

spirit – being exhibited to my mind in the Dissenters almost in caricature.' And it must be said at once that it seems both the Arnolds were right: this was indeed what Dissent had become – as distinct from 'what it had always been'. Thus Matthew Arnold's attack, it will be recalled, is focused on a newspaper, the *Nonconformist*, written (he says) 'with great sincerity and ability':

> The motto, the standard, the profession of faith which this organ of theirs carries aloft, is: 'The Dissidence of Dissent and the Protestantism of the Protestant religion'. There is sweetness and light, and an ideal of complete harmonious perfection! One need not go to culture and poetry to find language to judge it. Religion, with its instinct for perfection, supplies language to judge it, language too which is in our mouths every day. 'Finally, be of one mind, united in feeling', says St. Peter. There is an ideal which judges the Puritan ideal: 'The Dissidence of Dissent and the Protestantism of the Protestant religion'!

All the evidence suggests that this condemnation of late Victorian Dissent by the words of Scripture was entirely just. The *Nonconformist*, for instance, the journal that Arnold picks on, was founded and edited through forty years by Edward Miall (1809–81) who, originally a Congregationalist minister, was MP for Rochdale 1852–7 and for Bradford 1869–74. Miall retorted to Arnold obliquely in a House of Commons speech in 1871, advocating disestablishment:

> I wish to say something of the rural parishes of the kingdom. In each of these, we are told, the clergyman, maintained by national endowment, is a living link between the highest and the lowliest of the parishioners – is a cultivated gentleman, located just where there is, if not the greatest need, at any rate the best opportunity, for diffusing both 'sweetness and light' – is the fixed centre in the parish of civilization, of education, of charity, of piety – and I am told that I propose to abolish him and leave the people to fall back again into ignorance and Paganism. . . . These rural parishes have been in the undisturbed spiritual occupation of the clergy of the Church of England for generations past. . . . Well, what, on a large scale, has been the result? What are the most conspicuous characteristics of our labouring agricultural population? Do they include 'sweetness and light'? Do they include fairly-developed intelligence? Do they include a high state of

morality? Do they include affectionate veneration for religion? Are these the most prominent features by which the character of our agricultural population is distinguished, and in respect of which they bear away the palm from the inmates of towns? And the discouraging and painful answers to these queries – are they not to be found in blue-books, verified as they may be by minute personal observation?

This is effective parliamentary knockabout, but of course two wrongs cannot make a right; and the fact that in every generation perhaps the Anglican clergy have failed to be the *clerisy* that the idea of an Established Church requires them to be – this cannot mean that the very idea of a clerisy, as for instance Coleridge expounded it, is an error and a sham. For our purposes, that idea may be stated thus: since organization for public worship is necessarily a cultural phenomenon, religious leaders necessarily have a cultural responsibility towards their congregations, as well as a religious responsibility. That cultural responsibility extends, at some times and perhaps at all times, to the giving of political advice and political leadership. When the congregations are suffering intolerable economic conditions, such as the rural proletariat undoubtedly was suffering at the time Miall spoke (it was the oppressed and brutalized proletariat from which Thomas Hardy had just struggled to free himself), the responsibility of the clergy to give political leadership must take precedence perhaps over any other cultural duty whatever. And in Miall's time there *was* one body of clergy serving the agricultural labourer in this way. It was not the clergy of the Established Church, but it wasn't (either) the clergy of the middle-class Congregationalism that Miall spoke for. It was the clergy (mostly lay-preachers, in fact) of the Primitive Methodists, who supported Joseph Arch in his struggle to unionize farmworkers.

This is a special case, and not one that Miall had in mind. What *can* be said, however, is that, whereas the Anglican clergy are endowed and established precisely to discharge the duties of a clerisy, the dissenting clergy are not; and hence that when we find dissenting clergy none the less recognizing their cultural as well as their strictly religious duties, they deserve more credit than when we find a parson doing the same. In the first decades of the nineteenth century we find Robert Hall and his associates on the *Eclectic Review* doing just that, precisely as John Wesley did it for his Methodists, and as earlier still Watts and Doddridge had done it for Old Dissent. And small thanks any of them have got, from their own day to the present, from historians of all kinds and all shades of opinion!

However, by 1840 when Thomas Arnold wrote, still more plainly by 1870 when his son wrote, it is clear that the leaders of Dissent had almost universally and almost consciously abandoned any idea that they had cultural responsibilities at all. The proof is indeed where Matthew Arnold found it, in a career such as Edward Miall's. For Miall, the cultural responsibilities of Dissent begin and end with politics, and with politics on a deliberately sectarian basis, so that nearly all the political issues that Miall was heatedly concerned with now seem irrelevant and trivial. It is no more than just that all Miall's Gladstonian politicking brought him nothing that he was working for; for Gladstone consistently out-manoeuvred the nonconformist voters and MPs on whom he depended for his Liberal majorities – it was, for instance, a ludicrous miscalculation on Miall's part to think that Gladstone, that devoted High Anglican, was going to disestablish the Church of England and so give Miall what in 1871 he thought he was on the verge of getting. The nonconformists at Westminster drove Dilke and Parnell out of political life; and it is tempting to say that that seems to be the sum of their achievement.

At any rate, in *Culture and Anarchy* Arnold's harshness towards the dissenters of his day was abundantly justified. However, his attack on them in *St. Paul and Protestantism* was not. It moved William Hale White to unwonted anger in a footnote to his *John Bunyan* (1904): 'There is not perhaps anywhere to be found such a failure to discern the meaning of history as that of Mr. Arnold in dealing with Puritanism and Protestantism generally.' Arnold had contended that 'the Puritans are, and always have been, deficient in the specially Christian sort of righteousness'; and that Puritan theology 'could have proceeded from no one but the born Anglo-Saxon man of business, British or American'. The latter contention, little as it fits the facts of recorded Puritan history (not to speak of those well-known Anglo-American businessmen, Calvin and Zwingli, Melanchthon and Luther), has of course in a sophisticated form entered on a new lease of life, thanks to inaccurate popularizing in the wake of Weber and Tawney. How bad Arnold could be at his worst, when he is every inch what Bridges called him, 'Mr. Kidglove Cocksure', will appear from his address on 'The Church of England' in his *Last Essays on Church and Religion*. Here, too, he speaks of the dissenters:

> Look at one of the ablest of them, who is much before the public, and whose abilities I unfeignedly admire: Mr. Dale. Mr. Dale is really a pugilist, a brilliant pugilist. He has his arena down at Birmingham, where he does his practice with Mr. Chamberlain . . . and the rest of his band; and then from time to time he comes up to the metropolis, to London, and gives a public exhibition of his skill. And a very powerful performance it often is. And then, the Times observes, that the chief Dissenting ministers are becoming quite the intellectual equals of the ablest of the clergy. Very likely; this sort of practice is just the right thing for bracing a man's intellectual muscles; what I am a little uneasy about is his religious temper. The essence of religion is grace and peace. And though, no doubt, Mr. Dale cultivates grace and peace at other times, when he is not busy with his anti-Church practice, yet his cultivation of grace and peace can be none the better, and must naturally be something the worse, for the time and energy given to his pugilistic interludes. And the more that mankind, instead of placing their religion in all manner of things where it is not, come to place it in sheer goodness, and in grace and peace – and this is the tendency, I think, with the English people – the less favourable will public opinion be to the proceedings of the political Dissenters, and the less has the Church to fear from their pugnacious self-assertion.

Really, the impudence of the fellow! Is Arnold's tone in such a passage suffused with 'grace and peace'? And does he not realize that the tone of *The Times* is itself insufferable? – the dissenting ministers 'are becoming the intellectual equals of the clergy'! Two hundred years after Richard Baxter, and 150 after Jonathan Edwards, they 'are becoming'! We may well wonder if any dissenter, however benighted, could have been in 1870 more 'sectarian' in tone than this self-appointed champion of the Established Church. Moreover R. W. Dale, though he is a no more inspiring figure than Edward Miall and was for many years as closely associated with Joseph Chamberlain as Miall was with Gladstone, is in fact a figure of an altogether different order – notably, the only prominent dissenting minister to hold by the full uncompromising doctrine of the Eucharist in the second half of the century, as Robert Hall had done in the first half. And as for Arnold's own emasculated theology – 'sheer goodness . . . grace and peace' – we need only remember an Anglican of a later generation, R. H. Tawney: 'There is a distinctively Christian way of life. . . . This way of life is not, as appears often to be supposed, identical with what is called ''goodness''.' If in 1870 the dissenting churches make a sorry spectacle, what shall we say of the slackness of an Established Church that could invite Arnold to expound this supercilious milk-and-water to the assembled clergy of London at Sion College?

William Hale White who protested at Arnold's *St. Paul and Protestantism* was the same who wrote fiction under the name Mark Rutherford. No writer is more important if we are looking for what Dissent has been in English culture, what it is now, and what it may become. Accordingly, I want to consider Mark Rutherford in some detail.

> I like the Lutheran service, calm and grave,
> I like its ritual solemn and severe;
> The message of these bare and empty walls
> I bow to, I revere.
>
> But don't you see? Why surely you must know
> That for the last time Faith is with us there.
> She has not crossed the threshold yet to go,
> But all is swept and bare.
>
> She has not crossed the threshold on her way,
> She has not gone for good, and closed the door.
> But yet the hour has struck. Kneel down and pray,
> For you will pray no more.

So wrote the Russian Fyodor Tyutchev (1803–73). And one sees very well that it is the literary equivalent of the bareness and sparseness which Tyutchev responds to, that made the French Protestant André Gide exclaim enthusiastically of *The Autobiography of Mark Rutherford* (1881): 'I do not know any work that is more specifically Protestant. . . .' Moreover I have suggested that the same elusive but astringent quality is what we have to respond to if we are to value Isaac Watts's hymns and psalms as we should. All the same, D. H. Lawrence was not wrong when he remembered this book by Hale White as 'dull'; whereas if we register Watts's poems as dull, the dullness is in ourselves. In other words, despite their common ground and their common aesthetic, to move through a century or more from Watts to Hale White is to be conscious of a very sharp decline. No writing is less appealing than the prose of *The Autobiography of Mark Rutherford*; in all the honest and estimable book, there is hardly a sentence that falls upon the inward ear as memorable or shapely. It is not just that metre and stanza compel Watts's language into shapes that are harmonious; more cripplingly, Hale White explicitly denies himself any of the doctrinal speculations and expositions which time and again, in Watts as in Charles Wesley, make the paradoxes blaze from the page.

Six years later, however, *The Revolution in Tanner's Lane* (1887) is a very different matter. Though there is homespun awkwardness still – for instance a gap of twenty years in the middle of the narrative is very lamely managed – Hale White now permits himself at welcome points a rhetoric which there is little difficulty in recognizing as Dickensian, muted indeed but the better for it. And the book is the narrative not just of a human soul, but of a society, or rather of a society within a society – the society of English Dissent; for *The Revolution in Tanner's Lane* is a historical novel, as is *Adam Bede*, written by that woman whom Hale White knew in his youth and never ceased to revere. I'm afraid we are often not as careful as we should be about reading social history directly out of what are after all works of the imagination. Nevertheless in chapter XVI, the brilliantly sharp yet profoundly sympathetic evocation of the East Midlands community of 'Cowfold' – Cowfold that 'knew no poetry, save Dr. Watts, Pollok's *Course of Time*, and here and there a little of

Cowper' – is very plainly put together from distinct recollections by Hale White of accompanying his remarkable father on visits in the vicinity of Bedford, where he grew up. And so no one who reads this chapter need doubt that it is a vividly faithful account of how the sects were disposed in one not untypical provincial community about mid-century. We learn, for instance, how, if Dissent generally was the faith of the relatively unprivileged, within Dissent there were class divisions, in this case between the Congregationalists and the humbler Baptists.

The short narrative *Miriam's Schooling* (1890) is, through its first several chapters, the sharpest and wittiest of Mark Rutherford's stories. Yet it is a delicate contrivance, and must be delicately handled. Who will say, for instance, which way the wit and the irony are cutting when we read this of the heroine, early in the story?

> It must be remembered that although, as before observed, she was naturally truthful, she was so because she was fearless, and had the instinctive tendency to directness possessed by all forceful characters. Her veracity rested on no principle. She was not like Jeanie Deans, that triumph of culture, in whom a generalisation had so far prevailed that it was able to overcome the strongest of passions and prevent a lie even to save a sister's life. Miriam had been brought up in no such divine school. She had heard that lying was wrong, but she had no religion, although she listened to a sermon every Sunday, and consequently the relation in which the several duties and impulses stood to one another was totally different from that which was established in Sir Walter's heroine. By some strange chance, too, tradition, which often takes the place of religion, had no power over her; and although hatred of oppression and of harsh dealing is a very estimable quality, and one which will go a long way towards constructing an ethical system for us, it will not do everything.

Though Mark Rutherford is plainly being ironical at the expense of the Church from whose sermons Miriam learns so little, is he not being ironical also about the Scott who wrote *Heart of Midlothian* and created Jeanie Deans? We shall tend to think so, if we set beside that 'triumph of culture, in whom a generalisation had so far prevailed', a passage from Hale White's *Examination of the Charge of Apostasy against Wordsworth* (1898) where he says of the political radicalism of the young Wordsworth, from which he is counted an apostate, that it was a matter of abstractions, and therefore accompanied by 'the doubt which infects all abstractions, the suspicion that there are limitations and equally valid counter-abstractions'. The matter is of some importance because Hale White himself can seem to have been an apostate from the radicalism of his youth, and in vindicating Wordsworth he was vindicating himself.

It is possible to read *Miriam's Schooling* as a whole as contending that a mechanical and scientific education is morally more effective than literary and artistic schooling. Not only Felicia Hemans and James Montgomery, but also the music of Verdi and Shakespeare's *Romeo and Juliet*, are presented as doing nothing to remove the flaws from Miriam's character, something that is ultimately effected by the scruple and exactness of her artificer husband, and the clerical astronomer for whom her husband contrives an orrery. Miriam, to be sure, is very carefully presented to us as in many ways a special case. Nevertheless, the value of astronomy (which Hale White set great store by in his own life) is contended for very forcefully, notably in words given to the astronomer:

> 'Now,' continued Mr. Armstrong, 'these are the two great truths which I wish you not simply to acknowledge, but to *feel*. If you can once from your own observation realise the way the stars revolve – why some near the pole never set – why some never rise, and why Venus is seen both before the sun and after it – you will have done yourself more real good than if you were to dream for years of immeasurable distances, and what is beyond and beyond and beyond, and all that nonsense. The great beauty of astronomy is not what is incomprehensible in it, but its comprehensibility – its geometrical exactitude. Now you may look.'

It is hard to take this as anything but a re-statement at the end of the nineteenth century of the eighteenth century's 'argument from design'. In the words of the 'Ode' which Addison printed in the *Spectator* for Saturday, 23 August 1712 (thereby fulfilling a promise made to Isaac Watts four days before):

85

What though, in solemn silence, all
Move round the dark, terrestrial ball?
What though nor real voice nor sound
Amid their radiant orbs be found?
In reason's ear they all rejoice,
And utter forth a glorious voice,
For ever singing, as they shine,
'The hand that made us is divine'.

As elsewhere, so here, what Mark Rutherford utters in his generation is the dry but devout clarity of the eighteenth century. It comes as no surprise that he edited a volume of selections from the *Rambler*, and greatly admired Johnson – an attitude much less common in his day (when Macaulay's tendentious essay on Johnson and Boswell still held the field) than it is today. E. P. Thompson is finely judicious when he writes of 'Mark Rutherford, one of the few men who understood the full desolation of the inner history of 19th century Nonconformity – and who is yet, in himself, evidence of values that somehow survived'. What those values survived *from* was the cool and accommodating Dissent of the Augustan Age, not the heroic and intransigent Dissent of Jeanie Deans.

Mark Rutherford's disenchantment with radical politics is at its clearest in his *Clara Hapgood* (1896), particularly in chapter XXVI, a discussion with and between two Chartists, and chapter XXVIII, a moving reproof addressed to a Chartist by Giuseppe Mazzini. The book contains other good things – notably, an attack on Evangelicalism all the more devastating for being done in a tone of contemptuous geniality. However, the heroine never says anything that is not stilted, and her heroic sacrifice at the end – of the man she loves to her sister, while she goes off as an active revolutionary under Mazzini – is accordingly hard to believe in.

It was in Mark Rutherford's remaining novel, *Catherine Furze* (1893), that Gide found 'the so specifically Protestant qualities and virtues'. Of Rutherford's style in *Catherine Furze* one can indeed say, with Gide, that it is 'exquisitely transparent, scintillatingly pure', and of his art here that it is 'made of the renunciation of all false riches'. (Gide adds, incidentally: 'He is apolitical, because there is no politics without fraud.')

Very near the centre of *Catherine Furze*, which is set in 1840, is Rutherford's diagnosis of Evangelicalism, in the person of the Cantabrigian and 'Simeonite' rector, Theophilus Cardew; indeed the whole story, from one point of view, is the salvation of Cardew from Evangelicalism, and his 'conversion' to, in effect, Old Dissent. The conversion has to do with manners and with psychology. What is striking is that the psychology to which the Evangelical is converted is very markedly, almost obtrusively, of the eighteenth century. Conversely, the Evangelicalism from which he has to be saved is presented as Romantically subjective:

> The ultra-evangelical school in the Church preserved at that time the religious life of England, though in a very strange form. They believed and felt certain vital truths, although they did not know what was vital and what was not . . . Evangelicalism, however, to Mr. Cardew was dangerous. He was always prone to self-absorption, and the tendency was much increased by his religion. He lived an entirely interior life, and his joys and sorrows were not those of Abchurch, but of another sphere. Abchurch feared wet weather, drought, ague, rheumatism, loss of money, and, on Sundays, feared hell, but Mr. Cardew's fears were spiritual or even spectral. . . . If anything struck him it remained with him, deduction followed deduction in practice unfortunately as well as in thought, and he was ultimately landed in absurdity or something worse. He saw himself in things, and not as they were. A sunset was just what it might happen to symbolise to him at the time, and his judgments upon events and persons were striking, but they were frequently judgments upon creations of his own imagination, and were not in the least apposite to what was actually before him. The happy, artistic, Shakespearean temper, mirroring the world like a lake, was altogether foreign to him.

The eighteenth century alternative to this is first presented in chapter VI, in the persons of the Misses Ponsonby who, though apparently communicating Anglicans, are carefully said to have 'preserved in their Calvinistic evangelicalism a trace of the Cromwellian Ponsonby, the founder of the race'. It is in relation to their undemonstrative style of life, that Mark Rutherford reflects:

> We mistake our ancestors who read Pope and the *Spectator*. They were much like ourselves essentially, but they did not believe that there was nothing in us which should be smothered or strangled. Perhaps some day we shall go back to them, and find that the 'Rape of the

Lock' is better worth reading and really more helpful than magazine metaphysics. Anyhow, it is certain that the training which the Misses Ponsonby had received . . . had an effect upon their character not altogether unwholesome, and prevented any public crying for the moon, or any public charge of injustice against its Maker because it is unattainable.

However, the crucial confrontation is in chapter VII, and it turns upon Johnson's *Rasselas*, on which Cardew's disparaging comments are rejected both by the heroine, and by Cardew's admirable wife, whom he treats cruelly without knowing or intending it. Obviously it would suit my thesis better if the eighteenth century figures appealed to had been Watts and Doddridge rather than Pope and Johnson; none the less I take it that this is an oblique testimony by Hale White to my contention that, just as there is an often noted affinity between Evangelicalism and Romanticism, so there is an affinity just as close but seldom or never remarked, between neo-classicism and Calvinistic Dissent.

I have more to say about Mark Rutherford. And in particular I shall ask next time what it means for us to say, as we are likely to do, that his stories – however we may admire them – somehow don't strike us as truly *novels* at all. Unless I am mistaken, we shall be led, if we try to answer that question, into some very interesting speculations.

Meanwhile, however, I cannot end this lecture by permitting the attractive and admirable figure of William Hale White to conceal from us the depths that in his lifetime English Dissent had sunk to. The representative figure can hardly be other than Charles Haddon Spurgeon (1834–92), a name that I remember being spoken with veneration in the Baptist circles of my boyhood. For by the time the Metropolitan Tabernacle had been built for him, large enough for 5,000 sitting and another 1,000 standing, Spurgeon was minister to probably the largest congregation in Protestant Christendom. 'The boy preacher of Cambridgeshire', of Huguenot stock, son and grandson of Congregational ministers, converted, however, by a Primitive Methodist, Spurgeon joined the Baptists because he found the Scriptures supported the tenet of adult baptism. 'At the age of seventeen he was

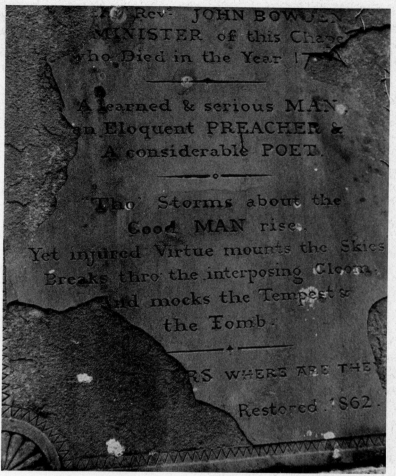

To Revᵈ JOHN BOWDEN
MINISTER of this Chapel
who Died in the Year 17..

A Learned & serious MAN,
an Eloquent PREACHER &
A considerable POET.

Tho' Storms about the
Good MAN rise,
Yet injured Virtue mounts the Skies
Breaks thro' the interposing Gloom
And mocks the Tempest &
the Tomb.

...RS WHERE ARE THE
Restored . 1862 .

1   Memorial tablet to John Bowden, Frome, Somerset

2   Pulpit, Lewin's Mead Unitarian Chapel, Bristol

3   Pulpit, Methodist 'New Room', Bristol

4   (a) Rook Lane Independent Chapel, Frome

(b) Gateacre Unitarian Chapel, Liverpool

5   (a) Friends' Meeting House, Long Sutton, Somerset

(b) Moravian Chapel, Malmesbury

6 Dilapidated interior of Rook Lane Chapel, Frome

7 (a) and (b) 'Graven Images'—Baptist headstones, Hanham, Bristol

8   Charles Wesley, outside the 'New Room', Bristol

invited to the pastorate of the Waterbeach Baptist Church and in two years he had doubled the numbers by conversions.' 'Though he was only nineteen when he began his ministry in South London', there too he had 'an immediate and almost embarrassing success'.

If George Whitefield cannot help but be one of the villains of our piece, still less can this be avoided in the case of Spurgeon, who a century later boasted, with justice, of being Whitefield's successor. The histrionics and sentimentalism of Spurgeon in the pulpit are hard to credit. And we must anticipate the objection that such vulgar effects were crucial to the effectiveness of Spurgeon's preaching, since his South London congregation was very largely the poorest of the poor – whereas for instance R. W. Dale's Congregational flock in Birmingham consisted of professional people, civic functionaries, merchants and manufacturers. Such an apology for Spurgeon cannot help but be offensively patronizing; and it is misjudged in other ways, since the evidence is that Spurgeon's vulgarities led him to misinterpret both the Scriptural text and Scriptural doctrine, and to let his exhortatory didacticism swamp out the sacramental aspects of worship. But in any case it is plain that from a standpoint concerned with the cultural implications of English Dissent, Spurgeon's ministry, and the influence he exerted, were disastrous; and that the appropriate *literary* memorial of Spurgeon's ministry deserves to be, what I suppose it already is, Samuel Butler's exasperated lampoon of 1875 (published in the *Spectator*, 1878), 'A Psalm of Montreal':

'The Discobolus is put here because he is vulgar,
He has neither vest nor pants with which to cover his limbs;
I, Sir, am a person of most respectable connections –
My brother-in-law is haberdasher to Mr. Spurgeon.'
                                        O God! O Montreal!

Then I said, 'O brother-in-law to Mr. Spurgeon's haberdasher,
Who seasonest also the skins of Canadian owls,
Thou callest trousers 'pants', whereas I call them 'trousers',
Therefore thou art in hell-fire and may the Lord pity thee!'
                                        O God! O Montreal!

'Preferrest thou the gospel of Montreal to the gospel of Hellas,
The gospel of thy connection with Mr. Spurgeon's
                    haberdasher to the gospel of the Discobolus?'
Yet none the less blasphemed he beauty saying, 'The
                        Discobolus hath no gospel,
But my brother-in-law is haberdasher to Mr. Spurgeon.'
                            O God! O Montreal!

Dissent in the Present Century

D. H. LAWRENCE, as is well known, esteemed Mark Rutherford highly. He wrote to A. W. McLeod in 1912:

> I've read the *Revolution in Tanner's Lane*, and find myself fearfully fond of Rutherford. I used to think him dull, but now I see he is so just and plucky and sound – and yes, perhaps I like his dullness – when one lives in a whirl of melodrama, as I seem to do just now, one is glad of a glass of good porter, like Rutherford.

This isn't exactly a left-handed compliment, but Lawrence's tribute to Rutherford is certainly hedged about with qualifications. Consider only the word 'plucky'. 'Plucky', rather than 'brave' or 'courageous', cannot help but be as patronizing in Lawrence here as it is, for instance, in E. M. Forster's *Two Cheers for Democracy*. Walter Savage Landor disliked 'pluck' and 'plucky', when they first came into use; and there is a valuable gloss on them in Angus Wilson's Ewing Lectures of 1963, *The Wild Garden*, where Wilson speaks of a quality embodied for him in his mother and repeatedly examined in his early stories about 'the resistance of many of my middle-class characters, particularly women, to economic and social decline'. This quality, Wilson says, is one 'to which the period and class English expression ''pluck'' most satisfactorily applied'; and he says that it 'commanded my deep admiration and compassion; nevertheless it also commanded my irony'. And it is surely true even today that to call somebody 'plucky' is to express, if not irony, then a degree of condescension.

Thus, without bearing down improperly on what is after all

only the unconsidered language of a slangy and casual letter, we may reasonably surmise, taking 'plucky' along with 'dull', that if Lawrence esteemed Rutherford he did so only from a distance, as exemplifying a moral stance that, though admirable in its way, certainly wouldn't suffice for Lawrence himself. And the point is of some importance because we are sometimes asked to think that Lawrence was especially well placed, not just for recognizing Rutherford's virtues but for locating them – in a cultural tradition that he shared with Rutherford, that of English Old Dissent. But I believe we have to question how far that tradition was in fact inherited by Lawrence, how far he had access to it. The document most often cited to show that he had such access is his 1928 newspaper article 'Hymns in a Man's Life'. There Lawrence declares: 'So, altogether, I am grateful to my "Congregational" upbringing. The Congregationalists are the oldest Nonconformists, descendants of the Oliver Cromwell Independents. They still had the Puritan tradition of no ritual. But they avoided the personal emotionalism which one found among the Methodists when I was a boy.' However, this is far from conclusive: it touchingly shows Lawrence aware that the tradition existed, but not that he had access to it, or gave it his allegiance. And the same can be said of the awkward and unfinished Rip Van Winkle fable called 'Autobiographical Fragment', posthumously published in *Phoenix*; there, too, Lawrence is careful to distinguish his mother's Congregationalism from 'the Wesleyan Chapel', but there is no evidence that Lawrence understood, as an experienced fact, the cultural and doctrinal differences which ground that distinction in something more substantial than mere taste. Moreover that admirable and irreplaceable witness to Lawrence's early conditioning, Jessie Chambers, is quite explicit that the culture which she speaks of Lawrence and herself as imbibing in the Eastwood Chapel was wholly a *literary* culture. It is quite misleading to speak of it as 'religious' except in the unacceptably broad and nebulous sense that Jessie Chambers intended when she wrote guilelessly to Emile Delavenay: 'Now all this feeling about the value of life and experience, and how the highest and best of it is embodied in art and literature, is in my mind . . . deeply and inevitably associated with religious feeling. For me, that *is* religion'. If there is any continuity at all between 'the Oliver Cromwell Independents' (those Calvinist Christians) and 'religion' as thus amply understood by Jessie Chambers, it is surely clear that the connections are altogether too tenuous to be dignified with such names as 'tradition' or 'culture' or even 'sub-culture'.

In saying so, I venture – not without trepidation – on to a famous battle-ground where the opposing forces were embodied in T. S. Eliot on the one hand, F. R. Leavis on the other. That historic engagement – and I speak without irony – is best mapped in an article by Dr Leavis, originally in *Scrutiny*, which he reprinted in 1955 as an Appendix to his *D. H. Lawrence, Novelist*. There Leavis recalls the account given of Lawrence in *After Strange Gods*, where Eliot had seen Lawrence as an extreme instance of the 'crippling effect upon men of letters of not having been brought up in the environment of a living and central tradition'. Eliot had spoken of Lawrence's 'lack of intellectual and social training' (as one might speak of toilet-training), and had declared 'that Lawrence started life wholly free from any restriction of tradition or institution'. And as regards Lawrence's mother, Eliot had referred to her 'vague hymn-singing pietism'. After rehearsing these bland judgments by Eliot *ex cathedra*, Leavis is provoked into an understandable but surely very unfortunate piece of chauvinism: 'It is when I come to these things in Mr. Eliot that I find myself saying: ''I am a fellow-countryman of D. H. Lawrence. Mr. Eliot is not. . . .''' The provocation is extreme; Eliot's tone is indeed insupportable. Moreover he is quite plainly wrong: Lawrence *was* brought up in an environment where several traditions were – whether 'central' or not (and whatever 'central' may be thought to mean) – undoubtedly in varying degrees still potent; and thus Lawrence *did* have both 'intellectual and social training'. Leavis is quite right to protest, with justified vehemence, at these comments in the mouth of the Missourian convert to the Church of England.

And yet . . . 'vague hymn-singing pietism', as a judgment on what Lawrence's mother transmitted to her sons, isn't anything that the historical records permit us to controvert. What in fact went on in the Eastwood Congregational church? That is information that we look for in vain, in Jessie Chambers as in Lawrence himself; and that very absence of testimony, from witnesses as eager and observant as those two, is not far short of damning. The fullest treatment by Lawrence of worship in that church is given (Leavis agrees) in the story, 'Fanny and Annie'. But that does nothing to answer what presents itself as the insistent question: Were the symbolic mysteries of the Faith, such as Lawrence the author of *Apocalypse* can be seen to hunger for, acted out in that church? And in default of evidence to the contrary, we can only fall back on the evidence of general practice in the dissenting churches of the 1890s – to the effect that the mysteries either were not celebrated, or were celebrated in such a way as to emasculate their symbolic significance.

And in that case, Eliot's 'vague hymn-singing pietism' is indeed just about what we are left with. We have seen in earlier lectures that, contrary to what the Anglican Eliot may have believed, it had not always been thus in the practice of the English dissenting churches. But how was it in Eastwood in the 1890s? Dr Leavis contends:

> the religion of Lawrence's mother does not deserve the contempt with which Mr Eliot dismisses it. The Chapel, in the Lawrence circle, was the centre of a strong social life, and the focus of a still persistent cultural tradition that had as its main drive the religious tradition of which Mr Eliot is so contemptuous. To turn, as Lawrence did, the earnestness and moral strenuousness of that tradition to the powering of an intellectual enquiringness was all in the tradition. That the Lawrences were Congregationalists is a relevant point – their Nonconformity was very far from being the debased tin-chapel salvationism that Mr Eliot appears to think it. Congregationalism had a peculiarly strong intellectual tradition. . . .

But alas, most of this surely is beside the point. The purpose of Church or Chapel is not to be 'the centre of a strong social life', but to be a centre and arena for *worship*, for the enactment of the ultimate mysteries. And certainly Congregationalism had once had 'a peculiarly strong intellectual tradition'. But did that tradition survive into, was it operative in, Eastwood in the 1890s? For lack of evidence to the contrary, I fear we must conclude that it was not, that the Congregationalism of Eastwood was as impoverished, intellectually and symbolically, as it was at that date through most of the kingdom; and accordingly that Lawrence may have been crippled from the first, and throughout his life, from having been born to, and reared in, a religious community that had lost its bearings and reneged on its inheritance. This is quite different from regretfully and impertinently underlining the obvious – that the grown-up Lawrence was never near to accepting the Christian Revelation; it is to question whether that Revelation was ever presented to him in such a form that, when he rejected it, he knew what he was rejecting. It is to the point to observe, as many readers have done, that Lawrence's characteristic rhetoric in verse and prose alike is much nearer to that of the Salvation Army or the Primitive Methodists than to the sinewy sobrieties of Congregationalism at its best. For that in Lawrence's lifetime we go not to him but to Mark Rutherford.

The loss by nineteenth-century Nonconformity of the sacramental and symbolic significance of the Lord's Supper is conveyed quite startlingly by Helen Corke on the first page of her *Lawrence and Apocalypse* (1933), where she recalls her own dissenting childhood:

> In the chapel, which is the House of God, sunlight comes dim through small coloured panes, staining one's white frock rose and blue. Here no one *eats*. Eating and drinking have nothing to do with God, HE is conveyed to my perception by the singing, the silences, the minister's oratorical tone, the presence of the Great Book.

'Eating and drinking have nothing to do with God. . . .' So much for the breaking of the bread, and the drinking of the blood of the Lamb! And a similar disastrous impoverishment shows up in Lawrence himself, in *Apocalypse*, the book that Helen Corke is commenting on. There Lawrence takes it for granted that Protestantism, and especially dissenting Protestantism, is a religion of individualism, of *personal* salvation. And because, so Lawrence maintains, 'the mass of men live and move, think and feel, collectively, and have practically no individual emotions or thoughts at all', the Protestantism of Church and Chapel cannot satisfy the mass of men, whose *collective* religion is articulated in

95

the New Testament only in the Book of Revelation, and in modern worship only by the Salvation Army. Lawrence could not have argued thus if the Congregationalism of his childhood had observed the Lord's Supper in the spirit of Robert Hall, as 'a *federal rite*' and 'a solemn recognition of each other as members of Christ'.

But in this as in much else Robert Hall is the exception that proves a sorry rule. The Baptists continued to preserve in its symbolic magnificence that one of the sacraments from which they take their name, but otherwise the decay of the sacraments in dissenting worship is a conspicuous feature of the nineteenth century. And this is particularly true of that central and cardinal rite, the sacrament of the Eucharist or the Lord's Supper. Ultimately the change is theological – the replacement, as in the 1833 Declaration of Faith of the Congregational Union, of a Calvinist or Lutheran understanding of what went on at the Eucharist by a Zwinglian or merely 'memorial' interpretation. (Thus in our century, the Congregationalist P. T. Forsyth, champion of renewed sacramentalism in dissenting worship, would declare that he held 'mere memorialism to be a more fatal error than the Mass, and a far less lovely'.) At a different level of seriousness but no less consequential was the insistence of Temperance crusaders in the later decades of the century that the Communion wine be non-alcoholic, and (still more damaging) the hygienic apprehensions which frowned upon the common cup or chalice, and replaced it by 'unbeautiful stacks of trays with minute cups, suggestive of the laboratory of a chemistry class, or . . . a doll's tea party'. As in the Barnsley of my boyhood, so today when I take communion in a dissenting church, I find the common cup, that necessary symbol of fellowship, replaced by the separate phials which cannot help but symbolize isolation. For how can I feel myself in love and fellowship with my neighbour when I confess, by the very form of the ceremony which seeks to announce such fellowship, that I'm afraid of catching a loathsome disease from his lips? Lawrence spoke, not without pride, of 'the Puritan tradition of no ritual'. But that tradition is being perverted if it makes us think that considerations like these are frivolous. For our ceremonial actions either have the sort of significance that I've just tried to illustrate, or else they have no significance at all, they are meaningless. Moreover, ceremonial actions *signify* in just the same way as works of art do. This is obvious in the case of such art forms as the dance and hieratic drama, but it is equally true, more elusively and profoundly, of literary art also – particularly of such literary art as Lawrence's own stories. For a symbolic and ceremonial act (or series of such acts) is as near to the centre of *The Captain's Doll* or *The Fox* as it is, more blatantly, in a late story like *The Woman Who Rode Away*. Accordingly, if Puritanism is to be saved from the imputation that it is the enemy of all art whatever, we have to repudiate Lawrence's formula, 'the Puritan tradition of no ritual', and to insist on the contrary that Puritanism implies ritual, but of a singularly austere and frugal kind. The distinction may seem to be a fine one, even lame; the difference may seem to be a difference only of degree. But it is not so, for to minds of a certain temper ceremony, whether in worship or in art, is more meaningful and momentous according as it is more austere. And if Lawrence came to think that his own hunger for ceremonial action could be satisfied only by the Salvation Army or (later) by Aztec blood-sacrifice, the blame may lie at the door of the Congregationalism he was reared in, which could have supplied him with austere versions of the ceremony he craved, but apparently failed to do so.

The same tradition failed Mark Rutherford also. And if we are less conscious of the failure, the thwarting, in his case than in Lawrence's, it is doubtless because in Rutherford's case there was less to thwart. Mark Rutherford (William Hale White) seems at first sight only another late Victorian who lost his faith, like Leslie Stephen except that, less clear-headedly than Stephen, he continued to call himself in some extended sense Christian long after he had lost the right to that title. In fact, however, more justly as well as more charitably, we can see Rutherford gradually putting together as much of the doctrine of Watts and Doddridge as could – so he soberly judged from first-hand experience – stand up to the conditions of nineteenth-century industrialism, as those conditions were experienced not just by the maimed derelicts whom the system cast aside but also by the factory-hand and the overworked clerk who together helped to keep it going. However, what Rutherford has in common with Leslie Stephen – what both of them share with atheists, agnostics and near-agnostics from their day to ours – is that both of them suppose the crux of the religious life to be the mental act of belief, not the physical act of worship. Accordingly the sacraments administered and received enter into their considerations hardly at all. Very telling on this point is a letter that Rutherford wrote in or about 1873 to his schoolboy son. The boy, away at school, had asked reasonably enough why his father, who called himself a Christian, never went to church. His father replied: 'The reason why I do not go to church on Sunday is that I do not know anybody who can teach me anything at church which I want to know. When I lived in London I always went to Mr Morris's. When I am in Exeter I go to your cousin's because I always learn something. . . .' Allowing for the fact that Hale White is here addressing a child, it is consonant with everything we know about him that he should assume the reason for church-going was to 'learn', to 'be told', rather than to *do* something. We've no reason to suppose that he took the Lord's Supper much more often than William Blake did, for whom 'mystery', the name that the Prayer Book gives to that sacrament, is consistently a term of abuse. And in the Congregationalist worship which White knew as a boy in Bedford, which he describes in hostile detail in *The Autobiography of Mark Rutherford*, it is a fact that the Lord's Supper is never mentioned. If in White's youth it was administered only infrequently, as a sort of optional extra, those Congregationalists were a long way indeed from Doddridge, author of the Communion hymn, 'My God, and is thy table spread', in whose church – as in Watts's also – the Friday or Saturday before a Communion Sunday was devoted to special services of preparation.

The lax or impatient ignorance which – even today, and even among dissenters – lumps together all the varieties of Dissent (as if Unitarian and Christadelphian, Primitive Methodist and Congregationalist, were interchangeable labels pasted on to one cultural attitude called 'puritan') obscures from us much of the significance of one undoubted masterpiece of the dissenting tradition, Edmund Gosse's *Father and Son*. First published in 1907, Gosse's extraordinary memoir of his father had been partially anticipated twice over – once by *The Unequal Yoke*, a short novel by Gosse that appeared anonymously in the *English Illustrated Magazine* for 1886, and second, by his biography of his father, *The Life of Philip Henry Gosse, F.R.S.* (1890). It was George Moore who recognized, behind the latter, another story that needed to be told, and pestered Gosse into telling it. In so far as *Father and Son* is now read and remembered, it is either as illustrating the clash between the Christian Revelation and Darwinianism, or else as a book to go on the shelf along with Samuel Butler's *Way of All Flesh* and Augustus Hare's *Life With Mother* – though both the latter tell of childhoods in Evangelical *Anglican* households. Yet Gosse is quite explicit about the particular sort of Dissent that his parents embraced – that of the Plymouth Brethren. Nowhere is this clearer or more pointed than in the intriguing account of how Gosse the schoolboy fell in with an elderly Baptist minister who turned out to be (or to have been) Sheridan Knowles, the celebrated dramatist; and how Knowles instigated the boy to ask his schoolmaster to read some Shakespeare in class, a practice that was abruptly discontinued presumably at the request of Gosse's father who, eminent scientist though he was, 'prided himself on never having read a page of Shakespeare, and on never having entered a theatre but once'. It is clear that in this instance the Old Dissent was less philistine than the New. And yet one of the great and unexpected virtues of Gosse's beautifully tender book is the proof it gives of how a culture and a tradition were transmitted to a child even within a sect so late-come and so rigid as that of the Plymouth Brethren. He tells movingly how he read a hymn by Toplady along with his mother, and how his father and he sang together hymns by the Wesleys – though not, to be sure, 'the hymns of Newman, Faber and Neale':

It was my father's plan from the first to keep me entirely ignorant of the poetry of the High Church, which deeply offended his Calvinism; he thought that religious truth could be sucked in, like mother's milk, from hymns which were godly and sound, and yet correctly versified; and I was therefore carefully trained in this direction from an early date. But my spirit had rebelled against some of these hymns, especially against those written – a mighty multitude – by Horatius Bonar; naughtily refusing to read Bonar's 'I heard the voice of Jesus say' to my mother in our Pimlico lodgings. A secret hostility to this particular form of effusion was already, at the age of seven, beginning to define itself in my brain, side by side with an unctuous infantile conformity.

A household like this, though so fanatical, cannot be called 'philistine'. A child who grew up in it cannot be said to have been aesthetically deprived. Indeed, a seven-year-old who can discriminate between the verse of Wesley and of Bonar is surely a sort of literary prodigy! And Gosse himself believed that appreciation of literature as an art began for him when he was eight, reading and studying with his father the Epistle to the Hebrews.

I believe we must conclude that every sect is a law unto itself, in the sense that each one has a unique relationship to the national and officially received culture. This is at least the hypothesis on which we must proceed, until we can take stock of the cultural bearings of each of them, even over a quite brief period such as the last eighty years. To take the Plymouth Brethren as an example, since it is what Gosse's book has brought us to, a history of their relations to the national culture in the present century would have to take account of General Orde Wingate, leader of the Chindits, killed in the Second World War. And among the documents that would need to be studied is Sybil Wingate's fugitive memoir of the religious culture in which she and her brother were nurtured:

Of the two great branches of the Christian tradition, the static and the revolutionary, my parents belonged to the second. I do not mean of course that they were politically on the left. Quite the contrary. In so far as they thought about politics at all (which was not very far) they might be described as Conservatives. But their religion was not of the type exemplified in all the great religious Establishments, Roman,

Orthodox or Anglican, whose function it is to inspire and direct the existing order of the world but not to change its essential character. Revolutionary Christianity, on the other hand, at least in its pure form, both desires and expects an imminent and total overthrow of the existing order and the substitution of 'a new heaven and a new earth', in which dwelleth 'righteousness'. Sometimes, as in 16th-century Munster, this attitude has flowed over into the directly political realm. More often it has confined itself to the religious sphere and has waited on an immediate Divine intervention. But the fundamental difference remains. Establishment Christianity, like the humorist, is broadly content with things as they are, and does not want a basic change. Revolutionary Christianity, like the satirist, is fighting a revolutionary war. Its cry is always 'How long, O Lord, how long' and it expects the reign of Christ upon this earth, and in the near future.

When we, as children, repeated the 96th Psalm, 'Let the field be joyful and all that is therein; then shall all the trees of the wood rejoice before the Lord, for he cometh, for he cometh to judge the earth; He shall judge the world with righteousness and the people with his truth', it was the field outside the window that was to be joyful and the trees at the bottom of the garden that would clap their hands. . . .

If we remember that Orthodox Dissent of the eighteenth and nineteenth centuries denounced 'millenarianism' as a heresy on a par with antinomianism and socinianism, we shall not need further proof of the deep and ancient, and principled, cleavages which divide one sect of English Dissent from others.

Sybil Wingate's testimony – highly intelligent as it surely is, and (as I find it) very affecting also – dates from as late as 1959. And it is not hard to find even more recent and formidable evidence of how stubbornly some of the irreconcilable attitudes of Dissent survive among us – to a degree that is of course never allowed for nor acknowledged by the confident pundits of TV or the public prints, when they tell us about the state of the nation. What persists is not just a system of belief but an intact sub-culture, with, for instance, its own distinctive tribal rhetoric. Thus, within the last ten years it was natural for a biographer of Charles Haddon Spurgeon to describe the hostility shown to Spurgeon at the start of his ministry by saying: 'Resenting the attacks made on his kingdom, the devil raged against the boy preacher.' And we may set against that the publication in 1972 of a book by an ex-President of the Congregational Church in England and Wales, with the jolly and thoroughly accommodating title, *The Puritan Pleasures of the Detective Story*. English Dissent is a phenomenon as various and as mysteriously unexamined as ever it was.

I am not competent – not I suspect is any one else – to take stock of this bizarre diversity, its broad quietist middle no less than its salvationist and millenarian extremes. Instead let us look for the last time at the Old or Orthodox Dissent, as the thrust of it, though sadly weakened and more than a little diverted, reaches into our own century in the person of Mark Rutherford. A recent critic has castigated Rutherford for 'luxuriating in epochal gloom', because he believed with Augustine Birrell that somewhere in or near the middle of the nineteenth century Old Dissent had been betrayed by its own adherents. But this is a reader (Valentine Cunningham) who is so little persuaded by Arnold's excoriation of 'the dissidence of dissent', that he can declare: 'Schism is a witness to the vigour of sectarianism: the life-blood of Dissent is dissent.' We have found reasons – for instance, in the weakening of sacramentalism in the dissenting churches – for thinking that Arnold's criticisms cannot be set aside so easily and boldly, and for thinking indeed that Rutherford and Birrell were right to discern a grievous loss of direction by Dissent in their lifetimes. What is at issue, as *Culture and Anarchy* makes very clear, is a strenuous *politicizing* of Dissent, gradually indeed but markedly, through several decades of the nineteenth century. We must tread carefully here, for Dissent in every period has fostered, and could not help but foster, a keen political awareness; and accordingly the leaders of Dissent in every generation – Philip Doddridge in his time, Robert Hall in his – found it necessary to take political stands, and give political 'leads'. Nevertheless, a real change occurs when in 1826 Robert Hall is succeeded at Leicester's Harvey Lane Baptist Chapel by Edward Miall's friend, J. P. Mursell; or when – to take another instance from a later decade – John Angell James in 1859 is replaced, at Carr's Lane, Birmingham, by R. W. Dale. With the extension of the franchise and the lifting of political disabilities from the dissenters, it became possible to organize dissenting sentiment into a powerful pressure group exerting itself first in municipal and local politics and then at Westminster. And the availability of such political leverage makes such late Victorian figures as Miall and Dale into very different creatures from Doddridge or Hall. For the achievement and exercise of this political power, a price had to be paid; and the cost is to be counted in terms of spirituality and culture. To Mark Rutherford, as to Matthew Arnold whom Rutherford so justifiably complained of, it seemed plain that the price paid was excessive. And this I suggest is the right explanation of the words that in his *Clara Hapgood* Mark Rutherford put in the mouth of Mazzini; for Rutherford as he grew older lost faith not just in the radical politics of his youth, but in all politics, in the political arena as such. To be blunt about it, though Rutherford wrote for the *Nonconformist* and was accordingly under obligations to Miall which he recognized, the career of a dissenting politician like Edward Miall came to be as depressing a spectacle for William Hale White as for Matthew Arnold.

And this is an appropriate point at which to risk the suggestion that Mark Rutherford's misgivings about Dissent as a political force have been borne out by subsequent history. For it is too easy to note that Edward Miall was out-manoeuvred by his parliamentary general, Gladstone, and to say that the driving of Dilke and Parnell from public life is the most that parliamentary nonconformity can claim as a political achievement. The nonconformist strength at Westminster was at its greatest not under Gladstone but under the nonconformist Lloyd George; and at least one historian, A. L. Rowse, has seen the presence of R. W. Dale, political ally and spiritual mentor of Joseph Chamberlain, exerting its baleful though high-principled influence over the administration of Joseph's son, Neville, so as to inspire in the 1930s the ruinous and bipartisan policy called 'appeasement'.

Leaving aside such an instance (admittedly debatable) of how politicized Dissent may have worked out in practice, the late a-political Mark Rutherford cannot help but fall foul of an assumption, very current among us and very much cherished: the assumption that political vigour is the same as cultural vigour, or at least that the first is an infallible register of the second. The history of English Dissent in the nineteenth century, as Mark Rutherford read it, disproves this cherished contention; and I may as well say that I think Rutherford was right. Those who cannot stomach this in Rutherford characteristically get round the difficulty by declaring, in Valentine Cunningham's words, that 'the autobiographical reference is the most important aspect of William Hale White's writing'. That is to say – and elsewhere Valentine Cunningham is quite explicit about it – that Mark Rutherford's books have value as personal testimony or slanted documentary, but certainly not as literature, as imaginative art. Yet it was as *art* that André Gide esteemed them. And the least we can do is to understand what Gide was responding to, before settling for the altogether more contemptuous assessment of Mark Rutherford which presents him as a more or less artless chronicler. And to this, to Mark Rutherford's *art*, I address myself in the few minutes remaining.

Francis Jeffrey, in the *Edinburgh Review* in 1804, distinguished between narratives that 'avoid all details that are not necessary or impressive', and the narratives of Samuel Richardson, with which, so Jeffrey goes on to say, 'we slip, invisible, into the domestic privacy of his characters, and hear and see everything that is done among them, whether it be interesting or otherwise'. Ian Watt quotes this in his *Rise of the Novel*, that masterly study which establishes how the Richardsonian method was in its time an astonishing novelty, foreshadowed only by some of the stories of Defoe; which establishes further how many factors worked together to make it probable that fictional narrative thus conceived should have been implemented just when it was, and not at any other date. Moreover, Ian Watt powerfully implies that fiction written on these principles, which he defines usefully as 'formal realism', has so dominated prose fiction in English in every generation since Richardson's that it is nowadays quite simply what we imagine 'fiction' or 'the novel' to be. This explains how it is that at the present day V. S. Pritchett can declare confidently in a review: 'Of course, Rutherford was not really a novelist'. For Mark Rutherford proceeds quite plainly in the spirit of those story-tellers whom Richardson superseded. From him we learn only those details that are 'necessary or impressive'. In the words of his biographer, Catherine Macdonald Maclean, speaking of his earliest narratives:

> such is the concentration on the theme, such the elimination of every particle of substance not integral to the theme, that at times these books seem rather to be essences than novels in the accepted sense of the word. In many respects they are more akin to poetry than to prose fiction. . . .

And the same can be said of Mark Rutherford's later fictions, such as *Catherine Furze*. That book, for instance, contains a description of an old meeting-house, which might be profitably compared with a justly celebrated description of what is in fact the Knutsford meeting-house, in Mrs Gaskell's *Ruth*. It is Elizabeth Gaskell's lovingly deliberate dwelling upon her description which does for us what we think a novel should do – it raises the place before our mind's eye, it 'takes us *there*'. Mark Rutherford's writing does not do this, for his is not an illusionistic art, as Mrs Gaskell's is. Whether he knew it or not, he was trying for something quite different from Elizabeth Gaskell, or George Eliot; and because his admiration for George Eliot is well known, it's particularly important that he should not be thought to try for, and fail to achieve, what George Eliot achieved. Ian Watt, who supplied the invaluable term 'formal realism', was the first to allow that it defines only one possible set of conventions for prose fiction; and the conventions that govern Mark Rutherford's fiction are not those, but some others. In the years since he died, more and more writers in many languages have abandoned the conventions of formal realism and tried to create, or to re-create, others; and a generation that can appreciate the fictions of Borges or Samuel Beckett should be well placed for responding to Rutherford's.

If this hypothesis deserves to be taken seriously, I could well be challenged to produce for this alleged relinquishment of formal realism the array of causes or contributory factors – socio-economic, ideological, psychological – that are marshalled by Ian

Watt to explain its inception, at the hands of the dissenter Defoe in the first place, and of Richardson in the second. I lack not just the opportunity but also the erudition; and so my suggestion must remain just that. And yet it is worth dwelling for a moment on Catherine Maclean's impression: 'more akin to poetry than to prose fiction'. For it is undeniable that by the time Mark Rutherford died, twentieth-century poetry was indeed set on a course like his, vowed to eliminate all optional superfluities; and it is not hard to imagine the Imagist poet, or the enthusiast for modern poetry in the Imagist tradition, who would take more pleasure in *Catherine Furze* than in *Felix Holt*. (Rutherford's story is, for one thing, so much shorter! And that, in all seriousness, is very much to the point.)

But one may think not of Rutherford's contemporaries, but of Daniel Defoe's. In particular, when Gide says of Mark Rutherford, 'His art is made of the renunciation of all false riches', how can we not think of the dissenting poet who protested: 'It was hard to restrain my verse always within the bounds of my design'? Isaac Watts's poetry has been described as an art of *kenosis* – which is a theological term, meaning 'the self-limitation of the divine power and attributes by the Son of God in the Incarnation'. Thus Harry Escott in his *Isaac Watts, Hymnographer* can speak of 'artistic kenosis', and explain this by saying: 'Watts had to lay his poetic glories aside, and dress the profound message of the gospel in homespun verse and the language of the people.' And Mr John Hoyles of Queens' College can declare in his *Waning of the Renaissance*: 'Classicism for Watts was a hard task-master; it demanded from him an artistic kenosis.' *Kenosis* may be an unfortunate word, because hyperbolical; but it certainly comprehends 'renunciation', being indeed the technical term for the most awesome and extreme case of renunciation that we can conceive. Can it be an accident that artistic renunciation, *kenosis* in this sense, is common to Watts, to the French Protestant Gide, and to the lapsed English Calvinist Mark Rutherford? Surely not; it represents, surely, an aesthetic preference and principle integral to the Calvinist tradition, and therefore persisting to inform such as Gide and Mark Rutherford, on whom the religious and dogmatic and (in Gide's case) ethical precepts of Calvinism had ceased to exert much if any claim.

If this be so, we are in the position of thinking that Calvinism in the person of Defoe fomented or nourished 'formal realism', even as Calvinism in the person of Isaac Watts adumbrated an alternative to it. And that should make us pause. What can be said is that Calvinism as a theological system was far more consistently familiar to Watts than to Defoe; and that if the *economic* morality of Calvinism fired the author of *Robinson Crusoe* (as has been contended, but also denied), the *aesthetics* of Calvinism are fulfilled far more clearly in Isaac Watts and, 150 years later – much more partially, but still discernibly – in William Hale White who called himself Mark Rutherford.

Though I see no need for a peroration, yet it is probably in order and advisable, now that I conclude this course of lectures, for me to say something about what I hope they amount to, taken together. I can best do so by reminding you of a point I made in the first of them. I remarked then that the word 'culture' takes on a different colouring according as we take it to be defined chiefly by socio-political groupings and patterns of behaviour, or by religious groupings and beliefs and patterns of worship, or by aesthetic proclivities, patterns and values. I undertook to concentrate on 'culture' in this last sense, by which aesthetic considerations have priority over others, though I allowed that in the nature of the case I should have to attend from time to time to socio-political and religious practices, since these obviously affect aesthetic habits and preferences. I hope you feel that I have kept to my bargain. In the course of my studies I encountered assumptions and contentions of a socio-political kind which I cannot but regard as tendentious to the point of being deliberately misleading. Not without difficulty I have resisted the temptation to expose these falsifications as I have come across them. Some day I may stray from my proper ground so far as to challenge certain received notions about the social and political history of English Dissent over the past three centuries – to ask for instance why, if it was right for Dissent to resist the pretensions of the Crown when the Crown's representatives were squire and parson and bishop, it is wrong for Dissent to oppose them now when the Crown's representatives are the bureaucrats of the Ministry and the Shire Hall. But that enquiry would have to be conducted in a tone more acrimonious than the one I have struggled to maintain, not always successfully, through the last several weeks. 'Simplicity, sobriety, and measure' – these principles which (I have suggested) are characteristic of the dissenters' art from Isaac Watts through to Mark Rutherford are also, surely, the principles that should govern exposition and argument. How to preserve them while not blunting the cutting edge of polemic, when polemic is called for, is no easy matter. But I have done my best; and I thank you for your attention.

Notes

Notes to Lecture 1

p.9 – *English Presbyterianism . . . had by 1800 dissolved almost completely into Unitarianism. . . . The significance of this development . . . very great. . . .*

IN LATER NOTES I hope to go some way towards substantiating this contention; for nothing in the whole history of English Dissent seems more important culturally, or in more urgent need of being pondered and understood. For the moment it will suffice to quote the admittedly partial reflections of the Congregationalist Bernard Lord Manning in 1937:

> There were in the century two main currents of religious thought. One was Arian, developing into Socinianism and Unitarianism. The other was evangelical. Leaving aside detail, we may say that English Presbyterians with a few gallant exceptions were swept on by the first current, losing their Calvinism and providing the foundations of the modern Unitarian denomination. Congregationalists were swept on by the second current; and to their Calvinism added Evangelicalism.
>
> Before we offer explanations let us dwell on the greatness of this achievement, an achievement in the sphere of spiritual religion *beside which the political and social deeds of seventeenth-century and nineteenth-century Congregationalism seem almost paltry.* In the day when Presbyterianism was destroyed by Latitudinarian and Unitarian doctrine, and when Anglicanism was riddled by it, our forefathers (after some sad lapses and desperate struggles) kept the faith. This was their first achievement as a tolerated church, and had they done nothing more they would have made the place of their pilgrimage glorious (*Essays in Orthodox Dissent*, 1939, p. 186, italics added).

Manning goes on to argue that one reason why Congregationalism remained Trinitarian was its possession of a Trinitarian liturgy, in the form of the psalms and hymns of Watts.

pp. 11–12 *Edwards's doctrine . . . has never been controverted . . . but . . . tacitly laid aside. . . .*

This seems to have already been largely true as long ago as 1901, if we may trust Williston Walker writing in that year about Edwards's *Careful and Strict Enquiry. . . . .*

> The volume was, till comparatively recent times, in extensive use, being esteemed by Calvinists generally an unanswerable critique of the Arminian position. It has met, however, with growing dissent, and though not often directly opposed of late years, is largely felt to lie outside the conceptions of modern religious thought; but it has acceptance still, especially with those who hold a necessitarian view of the universe, and may be said never to have had a positive and complete refutation, though suffering a constantly increasing neglect (JONATHAN EDWARDS, from *Ten New England Leaders*, in David Levin (ed.), *Jonathan Edwards: A Profile*, 1969, pp. 110–11).

Walker presumably has in mind chiefly American practices. In England the abandonment of the strict Calvinist position by preachers of intellectual pretensions may have come about gradually between about 1850 and 1887. That is suggested by chapter 7 of *The Revolution in Tanner's Lane* (1887), where the preaching of 'The Reverend Thomas Bradshaw' is Mark Rutherford's admiring tribute to what he had heard from the Congregationalist Thomas Binney in the Weighhouse Chapel about 1850 (italics mine):

> His discourses were remarkably strong, and of a kind seldom, or indeed never, heard now. They taxed the whole mental powers of his audience, and were utterly unlike the simple stuff which became fashionable with the Evangelistic movement. . . . They will not as a rule bear printing, because the assumption on which they rest is *not now assumed*; but if it be granted, they are unanswerable. . . .

What is at issue here is the vexed question whether a 'moderate' Calvinism is a possibility. So far as I can see, Richard Baxter thought that it was, and that he had worked it out; Watts and Doddridge thought that it was, and that they preached it; after them, Robert Hall and William Carey and Andrew Fuller thought the same; and in the 1830s William Hale White the elder, Mark Rutherford's father, could declare that 'a moderate Calvinism suited him best'. But if Jonathan Edwards has never been refuted, that must mean that none of these attempts to 'moderate' can in the end stand up to the rigour of Edwards's logic. Yet if it be true, as R. W. Dale declared, 'that theologians who begin with Calvin must end with Calvin', and if it follows (as it must) that all these compromise positions are intellectually disreputable compared with Edwards's, one may still contend – as Doddridge for one never tired of doing – that true religion is 'experimental'; that is to say, that it is grounded not on any chain of reasoning but on an irrefutable experience in the act of worship. And if there is no room for that experience in a logical scheme, so much the worse for the logic. However, this is very different from the awkward mish-mash of irreconcilable assumptions – Arminian on the one hand, Calvinist on the other – which was the legacy of the Evangelical Movement. And it was this, as preached from nineteenth-century dissenting pulpits, which brought the mere expression, 'moderate Calvinism', into such disrepute as it had for Mark Rutherford:

> They were taught what was called a 'moderate Calvinism', a phrase not easy to understand. If it had any meaning, it was that predestination, election, and reprobation, were unquestionably true, but they were dogmas about which it was not prudent to say much, for some of the congregation were a little Arminian, and St. James could not be totally neglected.

R. W. Dale said, of such 'moderate Calvinist' preachers: 'They might be assured that, according to the eternal counsels of God, Christ died only for the elect; but they preached as if they thought that He died for every man in the congregation.'

For Mark Rutherford the dilemma was exacerbated because he appears never to have been, in Philip Doddridge's sense, an *experimental* Christian. And so we find in him an eloquent nostalgia for the immoderate Calvinism of Edwards, which he was in love with though he could not believe in it. It seems to be this that lies behind an impassioned digression in chapter 9 of *The Revolution in Tanner's Lane*, when Rutherford reflects on the state of mind of his Calvinist hero, Zachariah Coleman:

> He admitted the unquestionable right of the Almighty to damn three parts of creation to eternal hell if He so willed; why not, then, one sinner like Zachariah Coleman to a weary pilgrimage for thirty or forty years? . . . At last – and here, through his religion, he came down to the only consolation possible for him – he said to himself, 'Thus hath He decreed; it is foolish to struggle against His ordinances; we can but submit.' 'A poor gospel,' says his critic. Poor! – yes; but it is genuine; and this at least must be said for Puritanism, that of all the theologies and philosophies it is the most honest in its recognition of the facts; the most real, if we penetrate to the heart of it, in the remedy which it offers.

p. 16 *'The years of Walpole's rule . . . years of spiritual desolation. . . .'*
When the Master of Balliol can within the last ten years dismiss early

Hanoverian culture in a few well-chosen and vindictive generalizations, we can hardly be surprised to hear from a church historian of thirty years ago, speaking of the decades after the Toleration Act of 1689:

> A cold fog of religious indifference descended upon the nation which for a century had been preoccupied with religious questions. It now began to think of other things, such as commerce and science. Religion was displaced from the centre of interest. The eighteenth century was an age of reason. The Deists whittled down the supernatural element in Christianity and reduced its fundamentals to the mere essentials of the natural reason. Philosophy became sceptical under the influence of Locke and Hume. Science made extraordinary progress and attracted to itself great attention. Morality sank to a low level and in all classes of society gambling and drunkenness were rife.

For this authority – A. C. Underwood, whose *History of the English Baptists* (1946) is in fact a mine of curious and intriguing information – there is the excuse that the denominations he is particularly concerned with, the General and the Particular Baptists, do indeed seem to have been sunk in lethargy during this period, though perhaps for reasons peculiar to themselves. In any case there is hardly a history one may consult that does not tell the same groundless tale. There is perhaps not much that the literary historian has to tell the social historian, the historian of ideas, or the church historian, but this much he has to tell them, and has been telling them for fifty years if they would only deign to listen: that the culture which produced and sustained Alexander Pope, a poet of passionate imagination which it is proper to call Shakespearean, just cannot be subjected any longer to such a repeatedly exploded pontification as: 'The eighteenth century was an age of reason.' The most intriguing as well as one of the most extreme statements of this position, as it bears upon Dissent in particular, is Maximin Piette's: 'With the prospect of struggles, tortures and hanging gone, life seemed to lose all its zest. For them religious fervour and persecution were things which went hand in hand. When one ceased, the other likewise disappeared.' Piette wrote as a Roman Catholic, and we may suppose him to be inviting the entirely just reflection that religious fervour which required such outrageous stimulants was not worth very much – which does not prevent the Baptist Underwood from deciding that 'Piette exaggerates little, if at all. . . .'

As for Pope, one way to explain away his fertile presence in an age allegedly sterile is to maintain that he could survive only in spite of his age and in tension with it – as an embattled Tory in an age dominated by

Whigs. This argument puts him at the opposite end of the social and political spectrum to the dissenters, Whigs to a man. But as a Roman Catholic, Pope himself was technically a nonconformist; and in Howard Erskine-Hill's *Social Milieu of Alexander Pope* (1975) there is an invaluable portrait of the Baptist financier, Sir John Blunt (1667–1733), who figures in Pope's 'Epistle to Bathurst' as 'Much injur'd Blunt', and Erskine-Hill shows how Pope's sympathies could reach across the sectarian and political divide to enter into the feelings of one who was an outsider like himself. The play of Pope's sympathies, we are persuaded, is as complex and subtle as a great novelist's: 'Blunt's paradox is like that of a later puritan businessman, Bulstrode in Chapter 71 of George Eliot's *Middlemarch*: he is guilty, but his denunciation of others' guilt is not less true for that reason.'

Blunt, who was largely responsible for the *débâcle* of the South Seas Bubble but was made by Walpole and the Court to seem *solely* responsible for it, might have been fashioned expressly to fit the Weber-Tawney thesis which links protestant Dissent with Capitalism; and accordingly it is worth pausing on him for a moment. It was not left for the present century to see connections between Dissent and speculative finance. A Victorian dissenter, the linguist and traveller Sir John Bowring, in his *Autobiographical Recollections* (1877) reflected:

> In the case of the Jews, persecution drove them from the ordinary pursuits of life to money-making and usury (I attach no disgraceful meaning to the word), just as our Dissenters, tormented by the Test and Corporation Acts, betook themselves to merchandise and manufactures, and, in both cases, the results have been eminently successful. The Rothschilds and Barings may attribute their present opulence to the sufferings of their forefathers.

But of course Rothschild, Baring and Blunt alike dealt in no merchandise but money; they *manufactured* nothing. (Why Blunt failed, where Baring and Rothschild succeeded, is well brought out by Erskine-Hill.) The distinction which Bowring fails to make had been made, with astonishing acuteness, in Pope's and Blunt's lifetime by the dissenter Defoe, in an essay on 'projectors'; and for an instance of a capitalist (a 'projector') whose activities were valuable and necessary we might take the London Baptist minister, Edward Wallin, who represented the inventor Thomas Newcomen on the syndicate formed in 1716 to exploit the patent protecting the steam engine that Newcomen had invented (see L. T. C. Rolt, *Thomas Newcomen*, 1963). Newcomen (1663–1729) was himself a Baptist, as was his partner John Calley or Cawley in their home town of Dartmouth; and it was Baptists in the Bromsgrove area who some time before 1725 gave Newcomen the chance to construct the working engine which, when he was forty-nine, brought him success. It is not only through literature that we discern Dissent as a close-knit, tribal sub-culture.

Another place where Pope appears to sympathize with a dissenter is in the 'Epilogue to the Satires':

> Let modest Foster, if he will, excell
> Ten metropolitans in preaching well.

This is James Foster, born in Exeter in 1697, who is said to have adopted about 1718 'the arian creed, though he at last settled in what may be denominated low socinianism'. After serving obscure and impoverished congregations in Somerset and Wiltshire, Foster moved to London in 1724 as joint pastor of the General Baptist congregation, Barbican. (That he was of the Arminian *General* Baptists is important.) It was shortly thereafter that he became famous. A manuscript of the time describes his 'evening lecture on the Lord's-day at the Old Jewry': 'Here was a confluence of persons of every rank, station, and quality. Wits, free-thinkers, numbers of clergy, who, while they gratified their curiosity, had their prepossessions shaken, and their prejudices loosened.' It is not what one expects to hear of a generation allegedly sunk in religious apathy and Erastianism.

Foster's celebrity was crowned when after the failure of the '45 he attended the Earl of Kilmarnock in the Tower under sentence of death for high treason. Foster subsequently published *An Account of the Late Earl of Kilmarnock after his Sentence, and on the Day of his Execution* (1746), which provoked *Kilmarnock's Ghost* (1747), an attack by Malachi Blake, dissenting minister at Blandford, and also a more formidable rejoinder from the appropriately named John Brine (1703–65), who took the ultra-Calvinist position of refusing to evangelize since to do so would be to meddle with God's absolute prerogative of election when and as He pleased. Bogue and Bennett in their *History of Dissenters* (1809), and Joseph Ivimey in his *History of the English Baptists* (1811–30) are sure that Foster was left without a leg to stand on; but they are all fierce Calvinists, so their testimony is suspect. All the same Foster was a dubious character, and it's not easy to see why Pope should pay him a gratuitous compliment. When Topham Beauclerk put the question in 1780 – 'Why did Pope say this?' – he was told by Doctor Johnson: 'Sir, he hoped it would vex somebody.' This we may be happy to take as conclusive. Yet the significance of James Foster for our present enquiry is considerable. His career shows that Isaac Watts was not alone in his generation of dissenters, in making the dissenting pulpit a rostrum for expounding and recommending the Augustan-Hanoverian cultural compromise. Where perhaps he *was* alone was in doing this while yet escaping – though by a hair's breadth sometimes – such divagations into heresy as Foster fell into or cheerfully embraced.

Certainly Johnson, who had as sharp a nose for heresy as any dissenter, and as hearty a detestation of it, was not likely to overlook the differences between Watts and Foster; as we see he did not from Dr Thomas Campbell's *Diary of a Visit to England in 1775* (Sydney, 1854; ed. J. L. Clifford, Cambridge, 1947), which records that 'when Mrs Thrale quoted something from Foster's *Sermons*, Johnson flew into a passion, and said that Foster was a man of mean ability, and of no original thinking'. Hester Thrale perhaps remembered Johnson's reprimand. At any rate she is to be found, long after she had become Mrs Piozzi and forfeited Johnson's esteem by the change, indeed fifteen years after Johnson had died, annotating Watts's *Philosophical Essays* and writing rather touchingly, against a paragraph by Watts: 'I *think* this was likewise Doctor Johnson's Opinion – I *think* so.' In the margin of another paragraph she exclaims: 'This is like Ajax's Prayer in the Iliad. O admirable Isaac Watts!' So far was Watts still, in 1800, from being read and esteemed only by dissenters and Evangelicals – he was studied still in solid Establishment circles, at least in those which kept alive the memory of Samuel Johnson (see James P. R. Lyell, *Mrs Piozzi and Isaac Watts, Being Annotations in the Autograph of Mrs Piozzi on a Copy of the First Edition of the 'Philosophical Essays' of Watts*, 1934, pp. 30, 26).

Among the dissenters of Watts's time there were many a great deal more outlandish and unaccountable than James Foster. One engagingly eccentric figure, of great consequence among the dissenters since she was the eldest daughter of General Ireton by Bridget Cromwell, the Protector's daughter, was Mrs Bendish, uncompromisingly devoted to the memory of her grandfather. We are told that she 'looked upon him as the first and greatest of mankind, and also as the best'. Widowed in 1707, Mrs Bendish survived until 1728, living mostly near Yarmouth. A Lowestoft acquaintance recorded, of this formidable lady:

> As the whole of Mrs. B.'s personal economy was not of the common form, her hours of visiting went generally out of the common season. She would very frequently come to visit at nine or ten at night, and sometimes later if the doors were not shut up. On such visits she generally stayed until about

one in the morning. Such late visits in those sober times, were considered by her friends as highly inconvenient yet nobody complained of them to her: the respect she universally commanded, gave her a license in this and many other irregularities. Mrs. B. never would suffer a servant to attend her – God, she said, was her guard, and she would have no other! Her dress on these visits, though it was in a taste of her own, was always grave and handsome. At about one in the morning, she used to put herself on the top of her mare, or into the chaise, and set off on her return. When the mare began to move, Mrs B. began to sing a psalm or one of Watts's hymns in a very loud but not a very harmonious key (THOMAS MILNER, *Life, Times, and Correspondence of Watts*, 1845, pp. 294ff).

It is clear that Mrs Bendish, vigilant keeper of the ark of the Cromwellian covenant, did not share the conviction, expressed by romanticizing commentators since her day and into our own, that Watts's more accommodating policies for Dissent represented a betrayal of that intransigent tradition. And for that matter Watts could be intransigent too – as when his loyal poem of 1705 to Queen Anne was given a vicious 'Palinodia' in 1721, because the Queen had let in the Tories ten years before; he would accommodate only up to a point.

Much more of a thorn in Watts's flesh was the notorious John Dunton, who was thought by some of his contemporaries to be not entirely, or not at all times, sane. This is the Dunton who wrote in 1696–7 a monthly paper exposing prostitution, *The Night Walker: or, Evening Rambles in Search after Lewd Women*, in which, according to Ian Watt, 'a virtuous purpose is avowed as strongly and as unconvincingly as it is today by sensational journalists engaged in similar appeals to public lubricity'. A vigorous and imaginative journalist like his greater contemporary Defoe, Dunton's lubricity more than once flickered suggestively about Watts's relations with the once-famous dissenting poetess, Elizabeth Rowe (1674–1737). Dunton's connection with Mrs Rowe went back to the 1690s when, as Elizabeth Singer, she published her early 'pindarick' poems in Dunton's *Athenian Mercury*. Some years later she is to be found engaged in a coquettish correspondence with Matthew Prior, himself of dissenting stock and a master of amorous badinage. Married in 1710, she was widowed five years later, and thenceforward applied herself to living down her early celebrity as 'the Pindarick Lady', becoming instead the Mrs Rowe who was famous throughout the eighteenth century as a protégée of Watts, 'devoted to pious works and devotional poetry'. Watts is said to have wanted to marry her, and to have warned Dunton to stop referring to her. How much he had to fear because of this relationship appears from the sneering *double entendre* in Edward Young's 5th Satire:

> What angels would those be, who thus excel
> In theologics, could they sew as well!
> Yet why should not the fair her text pursue?
> Can she more decently the doctor woo?
> Isaac, a brother of the canting strain,
> When he has knocked at his own skull in vain,
> To beauteous Marcia often will repair,
> With a dark text to light it at the fair.
> O how his pious soul exults to find
> Such love for holy men in womankind!
> Charm'd with her learning, with what rapture he
> Hangs on her bloom, like an industrious bee;
> Hums round about her, and with all his power
> Extracts sweet wisdom from so fair a flower.

From Young, a parson, Watts could not perhaps expect much else; but from a poet explicitly writing in the dissenting interest he might reasonably ask for more charity. How Dunton complied may be seen from his curious long poem of 1710, 'The Dissenting Doctors: A Poem on the Late Promotion of Mr Daniel Williams, Mr Edmund Calamy, Mr Joshua Oldfield, to the Degree of Doctor of Divinity.' (These doctorates, incidentally, were – as they had to be for more than a century afterwards – Scottish, not English.) The slipperiness of Dunton's tone is remarkable:

> Not Sleep beneath the shade in flowery fields
> To th' weary Traveller more pleasure yields;
> Nor, to assuage his thirst, the living Spring
> In heat of Summer more delight does bring,
> Than unto me thy well-tun'd Numbers do,
> In which thou dost both please and profit too.
> Born in a clime where storms and tempests grow,
> Far from the place where Helicon does flow,
> The Muses travel'd far to bless thy sight,
> And taught thee how to think, and how to write:
> 'Tis Doctor Watts, or farewell Rhyming quite!
> Thou dost not write like those who brand the times,
> And themselves most, with sharp satiric Rhymes;
> Nor does thy Muse with filthy Verses tear
> The modest Virgin's chaste and tender ear.
> Free from their faults, whate'er thy Muse indites,
> Not Ovid nor Tibullus softer writes:
> The choice of tuneful words t'express our thought,

> By thy example we have first been taught.
> Our English Virgil, and our Pindar too,
> In this, 'tis said, some negligence did shew,
> But you are Doctor to the chiming Crew.
> To thee alone we are beholden more
> Than all the Poets of the Times before.
> Thy Muse, inspir'd with a more pious rage,
> Did first refine the Genius of our Age.
> In thee a clear and female softness shin'd,
> With masculine vigour, force and judgment join'd.

This sounds handsome enough, unless the hyperboles – 'To thee alone we are beholden more/Than all the Poets of the Times before' – are made deliberately ludicrous. But despite the spattering of the page with Ovid and Tibullus, Virgil and Pindar, 'Doctor to the chiming Crew' may well be thought a left-handed compliment. We may well suspect, as we do at times with Defoe, that Dunton himself didn't know whether his tongue was in his cheek, or not. In any case we have read, a few lines earlier:

> The next Dissenter that does preach in Town,
> Who has no Titles got, nor Doctor's Gown
> (But merits more than any Doctor can).
> Is pious, learned, rhyming, modest *Watts*;
> 'He that did tune his harp by Chloris' notes;
> Nay was all ear, when on the banks of Thames
> He listen'd to her sweet harmonious strains;
> Listen'd! – and well he might; for when she sings,
> His zeal did rise on her seraphic wings. . . .'

with the footnote: 'Reader, consult Mr Watts's Poem to Mrs Singer, on the sight of some of her Divine Poems never printed . . . for your better understanding these five lines. . . .' When the self-appointed literary spokesmen for the dissenting interest were characters as turbulent and unstable as Dunton, or even Defoe, it was not without constant struggle that Watts could maintain simplicity, sobriety, and order as the distinguishing traits of his own life as of his poetry, and of the conduct he inculcated in his congregations.

With admirable loyalty, Johnson is solicitous of Watts's reputation on this vulnerable flank where his name is linked with Mrs Rowe's. For in a little-known review Johnson praised 'the copiousness and luxuriance of Mrs Rowe', together with 'her brightness of imagery, her purity of sentiments'. And he says of her and Watts together: 'They were pure from all the heresies of an age, to which every opinion is become a favourite that the universal Church has hitherto detested. . . . But to them all human eulogies are vain, whom I believe applauded by angels and numbered with the just.' This was in *The Literary Magazine; or Universal Review*, in 1756 (see Boswell's *Life*, edited by Glover, 1901, vol. I, p. 204).

Notes to Lecture 2

On the aesthetic sense of Calvin, and the aesthetics of Calvinism, see Henry·R. Van Til, *The Calvinistic Concept of Culture*, 1959, pp. 107, 109, 111. Brunetière is quoted by Van Til from *The Presbyterian and Reformed Review*, XII, 1901, pp. 392–414.

p. 27 *direct access to the culture which produced* Athalie
Doddridge's reading of Racine is recorded in a letter of 1723:

> Of all their dramatic poets, I have met with none that I admire so much as Racine. It is impossible not to be charmed with the pomp, elegance, and harmony of his language, as well as the majesty, tenderness, and propriety of his sentiments. The whole is conducted with a wonderful mixture of grandeur and simplicity, which sufficiently distinguishes him from the dulness of some tragedians, and the bombast of others.

In the same letter Doddridge recommends Fénelon, whom Watts also admired, saying that 'in his *Posthumous Essays* and his *Letters*, there are many admirable thoughts in practical and experimental religion, and very beautiful and divine sentiments in devotion'. On the other hand Watts no more than Bossuet could look with sympathy on Fénelon's enthusiasm for the mystical quietism of Mme Guyon; and we may suppose him to have that side of Fénelon in mind when he goes on to say that 'sometimes in large paragraphs, or in whole chapters together, you find him in the clouds of mystic divinity, and he never descends within the reach of common ideas or common sense'. There speaks the Watts who was a devoted admirer of Locke. (For the whole of this paragraph, see A. G. Matthews and G. F. Nuttall, 'The Literary Interests of Nonconformists in the 18th Century', *Transactions of the Congregational Historical Society*, vol. 12, 1933–6, pp. 337–8.)

Notes

As might be expected, the Wesleyans were less chary of Mme Guyon (and the Quakers, incidentally, co-opted her very eagerly). In John Wesley's *Journal* for 1742, we find him reading her *Torrents Spirituels*, and Henry Bett in his *Hymns of Methodism* recognizes imagery from this book in Charles Wesley's *Hymns and Sacred Poems* of 1749. As late as 1776 John Wesley published *An Extract of the Life of Madame Guion*. Cowper translated her extensively, but when his translations were published posthumously in 1801, his editor William Bull remarked with some agitation: 'To infer that the peculiarities of Madame Guion's theological sentiments, were adopted either by Mr. C. or by the Editor, would be . . . absurd. . . .'

A more extraordinary case of the French presence in eighteenth-century dissenting and Evangelical concerns is the career in English translation and allusion of a sonnet, 'Grand Dieu, tes jugements. . . .' by Jacques Vallée, Seigneur des Barreaux (1602–73), a famous libertine whom Pascal described as among those 'who would renounce their reason and become brute beasts', who repented, however, and died in retirement. The full story is extremely complicated, and has been disentangled by the meticulous and indispensable Henry Bett. It encompasses Watts's version, 'The Humble Enquiry'. dated 1695 but not published till the second edition of *Lyra Heroica* (1709); Addison quoting the French sonnet in full in the *Spectator*; attacks on John Wesley, by Thomas Church (1745) and Lavington (1749), for having adapted verses from the French: marginalia to Lavington by Mrs Thrale, ascribing the lines to the French source but with a crucial error; numerous reminiscences of the French lines in Charles Wesley's hymns; and a version by the Evangelical Henry Kirke White, 'Thy judgments, Lord, are just. . . .'

The title of Bishop Lavington's notorious polemic, *The Enthusiasm of Methodists and Papists Compared* (1749–51), hints at how anti-French chauvinism and anti-Papist prejudice could be mustered in some quarters of the Establishment against the often more charitable and cosmopolitan attitudes of dissenters and Wesleyans.

p. 34 *as late as 1960, a historian of Dissent*
Erik Routley, *English Religious Dissent*, 1960, p. 137.

Notes to Lecture 3

I quote Lucy Aikin from *Memoirs, Miscellanies and Letters of the Late Lucy Aikin*, edited by Philip Hemery Le Breton, 1864, p. 196. My quotations from and about Halévy's *The Birth of Methodism in England* (originally 1906), together with much of my information about him and his view of Methodism generally, come from the invaluable edition translated and introduced by Bernard Semmel (1971). The letter to Doddridge beginning, 'I will take this occasion. . . .' is reproduced in Duncan Coomer's modest but very useful *English Dissent under the Early Hanoverians* (1946). I have drawn also on Roger Thomas's, 'Philip Doddridge and Liberalism in Religion', in G. Nuttall (ed.), *Philip Doddridge* (1951). The passages about the Wesley hymns quoted from E. P. Thompson's *Making of the English Working Class* (1964) will be found on pp. 40 and 371–2 of the New York edition. All quotations comparing Charles Wesley with William Blake are from Martha Winburn England in *Hymns Unbidden* (1966).

p. 38 *Accommodation, yes; but at this rate? And on this scale?*
It was in 1737 that William Law told his fellow non-juror, John Byrom, 'that the Quakers were a subtle worldly-minded people, that they began with the contempt of learning, riches etc., but now were a politic worldly society, and strange people'. Seven years earlier Byrom had decided for himself: 'It is their life, their love of the world, their wisdom as to this generation, their luxury and neglect of that Spirit which they particularly pretend to, which I blame in a Quaker as well as in myself and others' (see Stephen Hobhouse, *William Law and Eighteenth-Century Quakerism*, 1928, pp. 119, 146). To be sure, 'accommodation' among the Quakers took a special form, since the external marks of it were a newly rigid observance of habits of dress, demeanour and address, which served to mark them off at a glance. On this, and on how nevertheless it masked a profound accommodation with the secular spirit of the age, see A. Neave Brayshaw, *The Quakers: Their Story and Message*, 1927, ch. XII.

Lucy Aikin, who quotes not from *The Spleen* but from another of Green's poems, 'The Seeker', had good reason to remember Green's poems, and to recognize their significance, for it was her own father, John Aikin, who in 1796 had re-issued them with an introduction that is still the most just and enthusiastic of all tributes to this poet:

He had not, like a Gray or a Collins, his mind early fraught with all the

121

stores of classic literature; nor could he devote months and years of learned leisure to the exquisite charms of versification or the refined ornaments of diction. He was a man of business, who had only the intervals of his regular employment to improve his mind by reading and reflection; and his poems appear to have been truly no more than hasty effusions for the amusement of himself and his particular friends. Numbers of works thus produced are born and die in the circle of every year; and it is only by the stamp of real genius that these have been preserved from a similar fate. But nature had bestowed on the author a strong and quick conception, and a wonderful power of bringing together remote ideas so as to produce the most novel and striking effects. No man ever thought more copiously or with more originality; no man ever less fell into the beaten track of common-place ideas and expressions. That cant of poetical phraseology which is the only resource of an ordinary writer, and which those of a superior class find it difficult to avoid, is scarcely anywhere to be met with in him. He has no hackneyed combinations of substantives and epithets; none of the tropes and figures of a schoolboy's Gradus. Often negligent, sometimes inaccurate, and not unfrequently prosaic, he redeems his defects by a rapid variety of beauties and brilliancies all his own, and affords more food to the understanding or imagination in a line or a couplet, than common writers in half a page (LUCY AIKIN, *Memoir of John Aikin, M.D.,* 1823, vol. 2, pp. 225–7).

Lucy Aikin declared that 'no one, I believe, of all his critical pieces was composed with greater pleasure in his subject than this'. And it is easy to believe her, for Aikin's own copy of verses in rhyming octosyllabics, 'Horatian Philosophy' – by no means a despicable performance – is quite plainly an exercise in Green's manner, and not just in the manner, but in substance too. As Aikin's daughter says, still speaking of Green's poetry:

> While the profusion of uncommon thoughts and witty allusions with which it is studded amused his fancy, the pervading spirit of the whole had much in it to attract his sympathetic approbation. It is that of a philosophy somewhat on the Horatian model, in which habitual serenity of mind is sought by a renunciation of the common objects of ambition, by temperate enjoyments and modest wishes, by the indulgence of a vein of free speculation, and by a general indifference and neutrality in the disputes which chiefly agitate the world (*op. cit*., pp. 186–7).

And the natural affinity between the Horatian frame of mind and the Quaker at its best, or indeed the Unitarian at its best, is something that deserves pondering, and perhaps study – for instance, as it bears upon a Quaker poet of our day, like Basil Bunting.

John Aikin is an important witness in any case, as the memorialist of those years, in the 1770s and 1780s, when the success of the Unitarian academy at Warrington shifted the intellectual, if not the imaginative, centre of the kingdom from London to an area bounded by Manchester to the east and Liverpool to the west. In both these cities the influence of the Warrington focus of intellectual endeavour persisted through several decades after the Warrington academy had been disbanded. Aikin's memorials of this 'vortex', and of the several personalities that whirled within it, are invaluable precisely because his own equable and Horatian temperament was not shared by his Warrington colleagues; and so our sense of their injudiciousness is gathered from a testimony that is at pains to minimize it. For example, what an unmanageable coxcomb Gilbert Wakefield was, is conveyed between the lines of Aikin's obituary tribute to him (*op. cit*., pp. 364–5), and is nowhere so unmistakable as in Wakefield's verses responding to the poem with which Aikin welcomed him from prison (*op. cit*., pp. 237–8):

> Next to that first of comforts to the soul,
> The plaudit of a conscience self-approv'd,
> AIKIN! I deem the gratulation sweet
> Of sympathising friendship, and a Muse
> Terse, uncorrupt, ingenuous, bold and free.

'The plaudit of a conscience self-approv'd' ('Self in benevolence absorb'd and lost', is what Wakefield modestly claims for himself in a later verse) very clearly characterized the Warrington Unitarian Jacobins as a group, Joseph Priestley not excepted. And such self-righteously self-appointed intellectual *élites*, usually ranging themselves on the revolutionary Left, have been a volatile element in English political life from John Aikin's day to ours. Aikin himself, though he pamphleteered in 1790 against Parliament's refusal to revoke the Test Act, was a more admirable and engaging person than the celebrities he chose to memorialize. And his daughter's memoir of him is, though an unexciting book, a worthy one. Nowhere in it, however, do we find anything to set beside what Lucy Aikin confessed to, in a letter of 1831 to Channing, about what it could mean to be brought up an English Unitarian under George III:

> the atmosphere of a sect and a party, which it was my fate to breathe from childhood, narrowed my affections within strait limits. Under the notion of a generous zeal for freedom, truth, and virtue, I cherished a set of prejudices and antipathies which placed beyond the pale of my charity not the few, but the many, the mass of my compatriots. I shudder now to think how *good a*

hater I was in the days of my youth. Time and reflection, a wider range of acquaintance, and a calmer state of the public mind, mitigated by degrees my bigotry; but I really knew not what it was to open my heart to the human race until I had drunk deeply into [*sic*] the spirit of your writings (*Memoirs, Miscellanies and Letters*, pp. 243–4).

p. 41 *Halévy . . . on this point . . . seems to be quite simply* wrong.
When Halévy seventy years ago, and E. P. Thompson more recently, saw the Methodist evangelists as doing for the dissenting interest what Hanoverian ministers like Watts and Doddridge should have done but didn't, they were only echoing what historians of Dissent have been saying since the beginning of the nineteenth century. Indeed the unanimity on this point is so remarkable that one would be frightened of questioning it, were it not that there is so plainly no agreed mark by which religious decline and religious revival may be measured. What is a sign of demoralization for one historian – for instance, Doddridge allowing Whitefield to preach from his pulpit – is, for another, a symptom of re-awakening vigour.

A clear example of the received opinion – and without doubt an influential one – is the second volume of Henry W. Clark's *History of English Nonconformity* (1913), wherein Book III, concerned with the years 1660 to 1736, is entitled, 'The Fading Ideal', and within that span the years 1714 to 1736 are called 'The Darkness before the Dawn', whereas the Methodist years, from 1736 to 1800, are treated of in Book IV under the title, 'The Partial Return to the Ideal'. If we look in Clark for the proof of these contentions we find that, though indeed he pays lip-service to such immeasurable entities as 'feeling' and 'fervour', his ultimate measure is not religious, certainly not doctrinal, but *political*; he is concerned for Church government, and for the relations between that government and the government of the State. Such matters are certainly important; but to look to them for the measure of religious health or decline is surely inadequate and even pedantic. Thus modern readers can hardly be expected to shake their heads in appalled revulsion, as Clark seems to want them to do, when he reveals (*op. cit.*, p. 166) that Thomas Abney, Watts's patron, as a London alderman took advantage of the Occasional Conformity Act. And Clark is even less compelling, appeals even more pedantically to a pristine Reformation principle which succeeding years had made inapplicable, when he tries to convict Watts himself of back-sliding (pp. 163–4):

It is worth while in this connection to take a glance at what may be called Congregationalism in a transition stage, as represented in the message sent by Isaac Watts to the Mark Lane Independent Church, when it called him to its pulpit in 1702. Watts had Congregationalism so to say in his blood; for his father was in jail for it when he was born in 1674, and his mother nursed him upon the prison steps; so that the son was from the first too much over-shadowed by the Congregational idea to travel as far from it as some were going. Yet, in giving some account of his views to the Mark Lane congregation, although he uses the old language as to every society of saints being a true Church, admits that a Church is not bound to submit itself blindly to its pastor's government, and admits also that in *some* matters a pastor ought to do nothing without the people's consent, he nevertheless declares that in the absence of a pastor a Church is 'incomplete' and without 'power in itself to administer all ordinances among them': there are various hints that the minister is something more than the *primus inter pares* which true Congregationalism holds him. . . . If one were unaware that such a tendency was at work upon a wider stage, Watts's words and clauses might pass unsuspected by, buried as they are among words and clauses of other tenor; but when one knows, then one discerns, in phrases slipped in here and there, how that tendency was claiming occasional visiting rights where it could not as yet hope to be made perfectly at home. And if Watts, for whom Congregational air had been mingled with the earliest breaths he drew, and for whom there was in heredity's cord so marked a Congregational strand – if Watts could go so far, one may conjecture how much further and how much more easily Congregationalists of less high and strenuous ancestry would be led away.

The strain of special pleading in this account is surely obvious; it provokes the retort that precisely because Watts knew at first hand or at one remove what persecution had meant, he had a better right than any subsequent commentator to decide when, and how far, to take note of the maxim *autres temps, autres moeurs*. One may reflect also that a pastor who has in his flock such black sheep as John Dunton is well advised to preserve some residual authority for himself and his office.

Moreover, with all his enthusiasm for the evangelizing of Wesley and Whitefield, Clark is forced to concede that two important dissenting communions – the Particular Baptists and the Quakers – seem to have gone through the eighteenth century largely unaffected by it. More generally, however, no one should want to deny that Dissent *was* affected, and in many ways profitably, by the Wesleyan and Evangelical Revival. This was not denied by R. W. Dale who, however, stands almost alone among historians of Dissent in maintaining that, if much was gained, much also was lost:

The Revival . . . helped to suppress the original type of Independent character. Reserve, a firm self-restraint in habits of expenditure and in amuse-
ments, patient, resolute industry, punctuality in the discharge of all obligations, a family life governed by exact method, a keen interest in theology,
and a keen interest in politics, a delight in books and in intellectual pursuits
of the severer kind, a strict Observance of Sunday – these were the charac-
teristics of the men who had been disciplined by Independent traditions. The
great Independents of the Commonwealth who had been formed by other
influences were freer and more genial; but in the course of a generation or
two the prevailing type of Independent character had taken this austere
form. Watts deplored the irregular habits of the Dissenters of his time; but in
many Churches the type was still preserved. . . . The authority of the
original type of character was still asserted by the public opinion of the
Churches. Any serious departure from it was condemned.

But when Congregational Churches began to be thronged with Churchmen who had inherited another ideal of Christian morals and conduct . . .
the whole spirit of the Churches was changed. The moral traditions of Inde-
pendency were lost. The gravity, severity, and solid strength, to which the
habits of an earlier age had formed the members of Congregational
Churches, disappeared. The intellectual earnestness also disappeared. Congregationalists ceased to be keen theologians, and they ceased to be keen
politicians (R. W. DALE, in A. W. W. Dale (ed.), *History of English Congregationalism*, 1907).

Not everyone will be so attracted as Dale plainly is, by gravity, severity
and reserve. However, by his account, what was lost was *culture*, or all
those elements of culture which go along with 'intellectual earnestness'.

It was George II who was for the dissenters, and long remained in
dissenting tradition, the paragon of princes; and the high-water mark of
the dissenters' royalism was when Doddridge and others were active in
1745 in raising levies to oppose the Pretender, despite the civic disabilities which debarred them from serving in arms in any responsible position themselves. George III, though the dissenters had high hopes of him
at the start, soon alienated most of them when he identified himself with
the policies of Bute; and for the dissenters, conscious of close ties with
their fellow sectaries across the Atlantic, the attempt to coerce the
American colonies was a bitter pill which many of them (in striking contrast to the Methodists) refused to swallow. The Baptist minister John
Collet Ryland scared the schoolboy Robert Hall by the violence with
which he declared himself for General Washington; and not many

dissenters could be as sorrowfully temperate as John Bowring – a Presbyterian, and grandfather of his celebrated namesake, the Victorian polyglot – when he wrote to his cousin in 1778:

> After the most deliberate consideration of the nature of the quarrel between us, I freely own it appears to me that they are right and we wrong, nor is there anything I more ardently wish for relative to our national concerns than a thorough change both of men and manners in the British Cabinet. Yet, as an Englishman, I by no means wish to see my country vanquished by the arms of France (*Autobiographical Recollections of Sir John Bowring*, 1877, pp. 2–3).

Thenceforward until the end of the century relations between the dissenters and the Crown were strained once again by mutual suspicions. Nevertheless, though the fact is seldom acknowledged, there were in this period dissenters who supported the national policies; and however it may have been earlier in the century, it is not true of this or of later periods that a Tory dissenter is a contradiction in terms:

> Dissenters could always be found who approved of the American War; who petitioned Parliament against the extension of Toleration; who supported Pitt and joined the volunteers during the French Revolution. If we find Richard Price, Joseph Priestley, Robert Hall and Robert Robinson on the one side, there were the Rev. Edward Pickard, the Rev. John Martin, the Rev. John Clayton and the Rev. David Rivers on the other (ANTHONY LINCOLN, *Some Political and Social Ideas of English Dissent, 1763–1800*, 1938, pp. 21–2).

In fact, of the four names cited here as belonging to the less than loyal Opposition in this period, three – Price, Priestley and Robinson – were, or ended up as, heterodox Unitarians quite unrepresentative of Dissent as a whole; and the fourth – Robert Hall, the Baptist – is ranked with them on the score of a couple of youthful polemics which he soon by implication disowned. Of the four 'Tory' names, the most interesting is that of John Clayton (1754–1843).

Clayton was at one time closely associated with the mercurial Sir Harry Trelawney, of the ancient Cornish family, with whom he took Congregationalism into Cornwall, itinerating from the baronet's family seat at Looe. How genteel Dissent could be at this period appears from an account of Sir Harry's being 'publicly set apart to the office of pastor or overseer, in the church of Christ, by the laying on of the hands of the Presbytery':

This solemnity took place at Southampton, April 22nd, 1777, with more of pomp and circumstance than usually attend services, when administered according to the simple forms of Protestant Dissenters. A large platform was raised, covered with green cloth, and a velvet cushion provided for the young baronet to kneel upon. Constables were in attendance, to guard against disorder and disturbance. The crowd, anxious to witness the celebration of the rite, under circumstances by no means common, was immense, and composed of all classes, fashionable and unfashionable, from the town and neighbourhood. . . .

Alas, Sir Harry later went Socinian.

When the Birmingham mob rioted against Joseph Priestley, Clayton preached a sermon, subsequently published, which – says his Victorian biographer – 'embodied some conservative sentiments, which would not be wholly endorsed by many of his brethren then, and still less now'. To this the 27-year-old Robert Hall replied with a pamphlet, *Christianity Consistent with a Love of Freedom* (1791). But Clayton was not to be deflected:

When the mind of the public was exasperated by party politics, and the horrors of the French Revolution made every ear tingle, and many hearts bleed, he set his face like a flint against what he termed 'the revolutionary mania'; and while barbarous atrocities were practised in a neighbouring land, and corresponding societies, treasonable plots, seditious libels, and furious demagogues, were in activity at home, he felt it to be his duty to insist much on relative obligations – especially those which refer to the subject and the magistrate. . . .

. . . he endeavoured to discriminate between the exploded doctrines of passive obedience and non-resistance, and that rational, just, and religious deference to constituted authorities, so indispensable to the liberty, safety, and prosperity of the empire.

The course he took proved offensive to not a few of his ministerial brethren; and to the whole fraternity of Jacobins and revolutionists, who rose up in arms against him, in squibs, pamphlets, and caricatures. . . .

. . . He tasked all his strength to stem the torrent of democratic fury (T. M. AVELING, *Memorials of the Clayton Family*, 1867, pp. 145–6).

It comes as no surprise that Clayton, professing these views (which incidentally were firmly upheld in the next generation from the pulpit of his eldest son), was possessed of private means – which at least takes care of any allegation that he was on the Government payroll. Moreover, by 1800 when he was minister of the Weighhouse Chapel in London (where Mark Rutherford was to admire the preaching of his successor,

Thomas Binney), his congregations were affluent and genteel, 'for there might have been counted at the doors of the Weighhouse chapel, from sixteen to twenty equipages, or full-appointed gentlemen's carriages, waiting to convey their owners, after public service, to their respective suburban villages'. What is significant is that his biographer Aveling, sixty years later, conveying this information, seems to speak of it as a phenomenon long vanished from the scene. It looks as if an audience for Dissent recognizably similar in social composition to that of Watts survived as late as 1800, but had vanished from dissenting chapels by 1860. If so, it may be that when it vanished it took with it from dissenting households the secular literary culture represented by what John Clayton read with his children (*op. cit.*, p. 100): 'Watts's *Lyrics*, Cowper's *Poems*, the *Odyssey of Homer*, as versified by that author, Pope's *Iliad*, and the *Dramas* of Hannah More.' Already in 1807 David Bogue and James Bennett in their *History of Dissenters* were very suspicious of Watts's versions of the Psalms, and explicitly lamented that Cowper should have spent any of his time on an author so unserious as Homer. Nineteenth-century Dissent was by and large to follow their lead, not John Clayton's.

p. 48 *no more incentive from within its ranks to relate the sub-culture to the national culture, than there is on the part of the Establishment. . . .*
T. B. Shepherd's *Methodism and the Literature of the Eighteenth Century* (1940), which might seem to address itself to just this topic, fails to live up to the promise of its title. It is particularly barren and perfunctory on the Wesleys' poetry. It has value, however, in directing attention to John Wesley's prose, especially his political and controversial writings like *A Farther Appeal to Men of Reason and Religion*. George Lawton's *John Wesley's English: A Study of his Literary Style* (1962) has more to say on this, but has the opposite defects to Shepherd's book, in that it stays unmanageably close to a card-index concordance to Wesley's works. In both these works may be found hints towards, and material for, a study of Wesleyan prose as carrying forward into the later eighteenth century, for the most part addicted to a more 'Corinthian' and ornamental prose, the easy, trenchant and conversational styles of Swift on the one hand, Robert South on the other – both of them masters whom Wesley appealed to and recommended. Such an investigation would be valuable.

Certainly what might on that showing be claimed for Methodism cannot be claimed for Dissent. By the end of the century dissenters were writing an English that is tumid and glittering; in particular Robert Hall, however estimable on other counts, is nowadays unreadable, though in his own day he was highly praised as an oratorical stylist.

Notes to Lecture 4

For dissenting magazines, see F. E. Mineka, *The Dissidence of Dissent* (1944). Olinthus Gregory's memoir of Robert Hall I read in *The Baptist Library*, 1843, vol. 3, pp. 225–78. For Elizabeth Haldane, see *Mrs Gaskell and her Friends* (1931); and for Augustine Birrell, *Things Past Redress* (1937). For Michael Faraday, see Henry Bence Jones, *The Life and Letters of Faraday*, 2 vols, (1870); L. Pearce Williams, *Michael Faraday: A Biography* (1965); and Joseph Agassi, *Faraday as a Natural Philosopher* (1971). I am grateful to my friend Robert Conquest for pointing out how Faraday's was a case I ought to take account of.

p. 66 *This Unitarian strategy . . . first evolved in the 1770s. . . .*
Dr Johnson would not have made the mistake which bedevils historians to the present day, of regarding Unitarians as merely the Left and liberal wing of English Dissent, rather than (what orthodox dissenters have seen in them) pernicious and alarming heretics. Accordingly, Boswell because of his own 'democratical' learnings cannot be trusted when he implies that Johnson was, or would have been, disconcerted by the Unitarian Joseph Towers (1737–99), in his *Letter to Dr Samuel Johnson, Occasioned by his Late Political Publications* (1775), and his *Essay on the Life, Character, and Writings of Dr Samuel Johnson* (1787). It is misleading to have Towers indexed in the Birkbeck/Hill edition of Boswell's *Life*, simply as 'dissenting minister'.

The same failure to distinguish the Unitarians from the rest of Dissent marks even an essay so learned and elegant as Anthony Lincoln's *Some Political and Social Ideas of English Dissent, 1763–1800* (1938). Here, having declared (p. 30) of the 'Rational Dissenters' (i.e. Unitarians and their fellow travellers) that, 'equally disliked by Churchmen and orthodox Dissenters, they formed a cultural unit remote from and above the Nonconformist community', Lincoln can none the less decide, with no awareness of inconsistency, that 'the history of significant dissenting opinion in the years 1763–1800 is the history of the Rational Dissenters'. The trap, of course, is precisely in the word 'significant'; Lincoln believes, along with modern commentators generally, that political opinions are necessarily more 'significant' than theological ones. But on that assumption there is no way to explain why David Bogue and James Bennett, or Joseph Ivimey and Robert Hall, or John Wesley and Samuel Johnson, behaved and wrote as they did.

Lincoln is a scrupulous historian, and he presents all the evidence for a quite different reading of events from the one he puts forward himself. (There can hardly be higher praise.) Particularly valuable are the pages he devotes to the matter of the Dissenting Application to Parliament in 1772–3. This is an obscure episode, and no one can be blamed for not knowing about it. And yet it is momentous for understanding the history of the dissenting interest. Lincoln explains the 'new situation' for dissenters, out of which came this appeal for a reconsideration of the Toleration Act:

> Briefly, that new situation was this. The benefits of the Toleration Act could be enjoyed under certain restrictions, the most notable being a compulsory subscription to all save three of the Thirty-nine Articles and certain portions of two others. Similar restrictions hampered dissenting schoolmasters and educationalists. *At the time of the passing of the Toleration Act, the Dissenters had been, for the most part, strictly Calvinist, with few objections of conscience to the Articles themselves* – so few that their dissent was represented by opponents as nothing but a contumacious obstinacy over 'things indifferent'. *So complete had been the revolution in beliefs of English Dissent in the century after 1689, that few of the Applicants of 1772–3 could comply with the subscription required.* Deprived of the protection of the Act, the position of the advanced Dissenters was, on paper at least, full of peril – a peril likely to become a very real one, should the intolerant enthusiasm of the Methodists ever penetrate to the Establishment.

Here the italics are mine, and with good reason. For the sentences italicized show how misleading it is to proceed – as Lincoln himself tries to do, as many since have done, and continue to do – as if the social and political attitudes of dissenters can be studied (in any period, but particularly in the late eighteenth century) in isolation from their *doctrinal* attitudes and convictions. 'Socinian', 'Arian', 'Antinomian', 'Unitarian', 'Trinitarian', 'Calvinist', 'Arminian' – pleasant as it might be to consign these labels to a realm of 'battles long ago', and of positions long exploded, no responsible historian can afford to regard them thus, since they represent principles for which (as the historical record shows) our forefathers would endure persecution and even martyrdom. Yet so conclusively have they been dismissed into the keeping of specialist disciplines called 'Theology' or 'Divinity' or 'Church History', that it will come as a surprise to many that the 39 Articles of the Church of England constitute a *Calvinist* document, and that at this historical juncture it is a body of dissenters whom we think of as the guardians of the Calvinist doctrines, who *petition to be freed from Calvinist shackles.*

This body of dissenters was, however, unrepresentative. The seventy ministers of the three denominations in London who signed the Application to Parliament of 1772 were wholly out of step with their brethren in the country, as they must have known; and as Lincoln very clearly recounts, it was in fact the provincial dissenters, still mostly Calvinist, who defeated the Application in Parliament in 1773. The consequences were far-reaching: the disunity of Dissent being thus revealed, the Establishment was emboldened to resist in 1790 the far juster demand for a repeal of the Test Act, a demand that was backed by the Calvinist dissenters as well as by the dissenters whom Lincoln calls 'advanced', the Priestleys and Gilbert Wakefields and Robert Robinsons, English *philosophes* who by their arrogance and intemperance thus queered the pitch for Dissent as a whole, permitting the Establishment to pretend for the benefit of the mobs of the 1790s that 'dissenter' meant the same as 'republican' and 'Jacobin'.

This is not the account of these matters that is commonly given by historians of a 'liberal' or 'radical' cast. And indeed I have nowhere seen it plainly asserted that the Arianism of Priestley did far more damage to Dissent than either the hostility of the Establishment or the ambiguous fervour of Methodism. Yet that seems to be the case, and it was moreover damage to dissenting *culture*, for the unabashed philistinism which appears in dissenters of the Regency like Bogue and Bennett, or Joseph Ivimey, quite plainly arises from the reflection that if liberal and philosophical reading leads to Utopian Jacobinism, and to denying the divinity of Christ and the efficacy of the Atonement, then such reading and such interests are what a dissenter must be dissuaded from.

Joseph Priestley himself was perhaps a great man, and a brave one. A more instructively ambiguous figure is Robert Robinson, born at Swaffham in 1734. Anthony Lincoln puts Robinson's *Arcana* of 1773 alongside Furneaux's *Letters to Blackstone* as 'one of the two ablest performances in the literature of Repeal'. 'It surrounds', he says, 'the events of 1772–3 with an atmosphere that can only be described as political romanticism'. And this is meant to be complimentary:

> There is a romantic strain purely English in some dissenting authors of this period, for already Romance was walking in the gardens of England. The personal character and literary qualities of Robert Robinson reveal this blend of candour and sensibility into a humane rationalism. . . .

Robinson, who went on to be Baptist pastor in Cambridge, and to have his biography written by the poet George Dyer, was not always viewed so indulgently. Joseph Ivimey in 1830 in the last volume of his *History of the English Baptists* decided:

> It is not possible to read the memoirs of this celebrated man without perceiving that Mr Robinson became a trifler in regard to serious things, and sceptical as respected the peculiar doctrines of christianity. At first pleading for the innocency of mental error, he was soon found proceeding in the high road towards Socinianism, which he ultimately reached; and, if Dr. Priestley is to be credited, but for this conciliatory scheme, would not have stopped till he had arrived at the dreary regions of infidelity.
>
> It seems almost incredible that the man who at one period of his life wrote the hymns, 'Jesus, lover of my soul', &c. 'Come thou fount of every blessing', &c. and 'Mighty God, while angels bless thee', &c. should have sunk so low as to revile the scripture doctrines of the Trinity and other corresponding truths.

And after quoting from Dyer's *Memoir*, Ivimey observes:

> The concluding part of Mr Robinson's history is indeed most affecting; and there is no way of considering it with any hope respecting his salvation, but that in which the late Dr. Abraham Rees once expressed himself to the writer of this article, that for some time before his death he was evidently *insane*!

Robinson was certainly exceptional, in that he found his way to Priestleyan 'liberalism' from, of all unlikely quarters, the Particular Baptists, and in Cambridge he took a lot of his Baptist flock with him. Robert Hall, when he succeeded Robinson in 1791, was not able to herd all the Cambridge Baptists back into orthodoxy. Incidentally, William Wordsworth's possession of Dyer's book about Robinson has been adduced to support contentions about the later Wordsworth's religious sentiments, which an accurate idea of what Robinson stood for will by no means bear out.

How the parliamentary events of 1772–3 may be presented – by one who wants to make the new Presbyterians as much part of Dissent as their Calvinist forebears had been – can be seen from Henry W. Clark's *History of English Nonconformity* (vol. 2, 1913):

> It must be confessed . . . that some non-Presbyterian Nonconformists objected to the Bill granting relief from subscription on the ground that Socinianism would flourish more luxuriantly if the restraints of subscription were removed. Even some who were in favour of the projected change complained that a false colour was being given to the matter by Presbyterian, otherwise Socinian, haste. It is abundantly evident that Presbyterians were far swifter in the race than were the rest. The whole position is perhaps fairly and adequately summed up by saying that in all these things the Presbyterians moved because they were glad and eager to move, while other Nonconformists moved because they must.

But this summary is neither 'fair' nor 'adequate' if it glosses over (as it does) the fact that Presbyterians were potentially and sometimes explicitly republican, whereas the rest of Dissent remained monarchist; nor if it glosses over (as it does) the hostility and resentment felt for the Socinian Presbyterians (or Unitarians – the terms are interchangeable) by the orthodox dissenters. That this was true not only of Calvinist zealots like Bogue and Bennett, but of a moderate like Robert Hall, can be seen from Hall's article in the *Eclectic Review* on Thomas Belsham's *Memoirs of the Late Rev. Theophilus Lindsey* (1812).

p.67   *as Elizabeth Haldane remarks. . . .*

The superciliousness of the Unitarians is at its most artlessly revealing in the case of Anna Laetitia Aikin, the famous Mrs Barbauld, whose career in the preceding generation set the pattern for both Elizabeth Gaskell and Harriet Martineau. In an extraordinary essay of 1775, Mrs Barbauld declared: 'It is the character of the present age to allow little to sentiment, and all the warm and generous emotions are to be treated as romantic by the supercilious brow of a cold-hearted philosophy.' It is not what we are likely to think of the age that produced Ossian and *The Man of Feeling*. And Mrs Barbauld herself realizes that in so far as 'cold-hearted philosophy' *was* characteristic of the Unitarian Warrington where she had grown up, to just that extent Warrington was out of step with its age. She wants to bring it into step, by adumbrating a characteristically Unitarian *devotion* which shall 'warm' the system of Unitarian belief, and the habits of Unitarian conduct. (Her essay has the title 'Thoughts on the Devotional Taste, and on Sects and Establishments'.) 'Warm', however, is what the Methodists are; and Mrs Barbauld has every sympathy with her Unitarian man of science who, observing what happens at Methodist meetings, decides that devotion had best be left 'to some florid declaimer who professes to work upon the passions of the lower class, where they are so debased by noise and nonsense, that it is no wonder if they move disgust in those of elegant and better-informed minds'. There is, however – Mrs Barbauld urges – 'a devotion, generous, liberal, and humane, the child of more exalted feelings than base minds can enter into'. The 'base minds' of 'the lower class' being thus denied the bare *possibility* of that Christian devotion which the Wesleys were inviting them to (as, of course, parson and pastor had invited them over the years), what must be our astonishment to find Mrs Barbauld and all the Aikins, indeed Unitarians in general, abrogating to themselves the title of 'Democrat' on the basis of having pro-American and later pro-French and of course pro-Negro sympathies! It was the bare-faced impudence of this manoeuvre that made the aged Horace Walpole change his mind about Mrs Barbauld (whom at her debut he had befriended) and in 1791 to explode in indignation, accusing her under the name of 'Deborah', in a letter to Hannah More:

> As I have not your aspen conscience, I cannot forgive the heart of a woman that is party per pale blood and tenderness, that curses our clergy and feels for negroes. Can I forget the 14th of July, when they all contributed their faggot to the fires that her presbytyrants (as Lord Melcombe called them) tried to light in every Smithfield in the island; and which, as Price and Priestley applauded in France, it would be folly to suppose they did not only wish, but meant to kindle here? Were they ignorant of the atrocious barbarities, injustice, and violation of oaths committed in France? Did Priestley not know that the clergy there had no option but between starving and perjury? . . . No, my good friend: *Deborah* may cant rhymes of compassion, but she is a hypocrite; and you shall not make me read her, nor, with all your sympathy and candour, can you esteem her. *Your* compassion for the poor blacks is genuine, sincere from your soul, most amiable; hers a measure of faction (Walpole's *Letters*, edited by P. Cunningham, 1906, IX, p. 354).

Mrs Barbauld's modern biographer, Betsy Rodgers (*Georgian Chronicle*, 1958, p. 112) is, whether she knows it or not, perpetuating an old and successful deception when she speaks, in relation to this letter from Walpole, of 'his dislike of Dissenters'. Priestley and Price and the Aikins, though they took care to act as if they spoke for Dissent in general, in fact spoke only for that small but influential minority which characteristically pretended to be Presbyterian while being in fact Arian and Unitarian.

Notes

Notes to Lecture 5

The critic whom I take to be wrong about George Eliot's Bulstrode is
Martin J. Svaglic, 'Religion in the Novels of George Eliot', *Journal of
English and Germanic Philology* (1954), reprinted in G. S. Haight (ed.),
A Century of George Eliot Criticism (1965). For Thomas and Matthew
Arnold, and Miall's parliamentary reply to the latter, see David M.
Thompson (ed.), *Nonconformity in the Nineteenth Century* (1972).
The verses of Tyutchev I quote in the translation by Frances Cornford
and Esther Polianowsky Salaman (1943).

p. 78 *It must be said at once that it seems both the Arnolds were
right. . . .*
Thirty years after he had collaborated with David Bogue on *The History
of Dissenters from the Revolution in 1688, to the Year 1808,* James
Bennett, the survivor of the partnership, brought the History up to date
with *The History of Dissenters During the Last Thirty Years* (1839).
And it is evident that the lapse of years had done nothing to moderate – if
anything, it had intensified – the savagely suspicious philistinism of the
earlier work. To a mind of this temper Robert Hall could not help but be
highly suspect. And in fact Bennett's account of Hall is astonishing in its
virulence:

> The humble estimate that he formed of himself and his own works, was not
> mere self-depreciation, but the sentence of sound wisdom. For he was distin-
> guished for taste rather than genius; and excelled in the power of adorning,
> but not of eliciting truth. Nothing like discovery in mental, moral or theo-
> logical science is to be found in his works, nor any remarkable proof of intel-
> lectual vigour in the highest sense. Some of his most splendid pages are imi-
> tations, though plagiarisms they cannot be called; because he so transmuted,
> and adorned, and improved what he borrowed, as to give him a right to call it
> his own. His exquisite sensibility to the sublime and beautiful in composi-
> tion, induced a lofty ambition to excel, which rendered his preparations for
> the press most laborious, but left him, after all, sincerely dissatisfied with the
> result; and offended, rather than gratified, by the extravagant praise which
> his better judgment told him was not true. He wrought into his sentences
> the trains of thought which led others, as well as himself, to his own conclu-
> sions; but which strike the reader as new, because he does not perceive them
> in the writings of those who are less ambitious of obtaining the approbation
> of cultivated minds. As a preacher to the literati, he stood alone; but this
> class of hearers is small, and is usually too conceited to be edified.

So much for 'cultivated minds'! They make up a class that is 'small, and . . . usually too conceited to be edified'. The espousal of philistinism could hardly be more explicit. Bennett goes on:

> Consciousness of the true character of his mind, led to the miscellaneous and fugitive nature of Mr Hall's works: for, had he attempted a treatise on any great and difficult theme, it would have demonstrated that he was not formed to extricate truth from the involutions that have embarrassed even lofty minds; but was the painter, or the poet, rather than the architect of moral and religious science. . . .
>
> His writings, therefore, are not destined, like those of Edwards, whom he admired . . . to instruct posterity; but if they are not suffered to lie on the shelf neglected, they will be taken down to rub off the rust, contracted by dealing largely in the compositions of those who valued thoughts as the sons of heaven, and despised words as the daughters of earth.

Bennett, we perceive, is a male chauvinist. But otherwise, this is substantially not unfair: Hall's literary style *is* meretricious; and his works *do* deserve to lie on the shelf unread, whereas Jonathan Edwards can never cease to fascinate and instruct. But Bennett's revealing distinction – 'the painter, or the poet, rather than the architect' shows that even if Hall had been as good a writer as his age thought him to be, Bennett's verdict would have been the same. This is unmistakable, from the final sentences of his account of Hall:

> Such rarities are, however, fraught with as much danger to the Christian, as benefit to the world. To the communion of which he was a bright ornament, Mr Hall's example would be pernicious, if it led to imitation; for, whatever admiration may be extorted by his printed compositions, it is not in this style that the Gospel should be preached. The rude simplicity of their Bunyan, would secure to the Baptists more effectually the highest honours of usefulness, than the elaborate eloquence of their Hall.

It is *all* the graces of language, not just Robert Hall's, that James Bennett is suspicious of. And accordingly we find him elsewhere explaining, with unmistakable satisfaction (*op. cit*., p. 306): 'The reading of Dissenters themselves, is very much limited to religious books; for being neither men of leisure nor of wealth, few of them go beyond their favourite hallowed circle. The frequency of preaching among them, and of devotional meetings, leaves them little opportunity, or desire, for a more extensive range.' For conclusive proof of Thomas Arnold's allegation – 'narrowness of view, and a want of learning and a sound critical spirit' – we need go only a few pages further:

If it be observed, as naturally it may, that the literary mediocrity of most of these publications, says little for the learning or genius of Dissenters; though this is not the object to be proved in a chapter on the state of religion, it may be replied, that the Son of God, when on earth, never visited Athens, to eclipse its philosophers, or Rome, to compete with her orators; but showed the superiority of his character, by confining himself to the paramount interests of eternity, which will retain their worth 'when tongues shall cease, and knowledge shall vanish away'.

This is the voice of that Evangelicalism which, by the received account, rescued eighteenth-century Dissent from stupor and sterility!

It is recognizably the same voice which, thirty years before when Bennett was collaborating with David Bogue, had declared of Isaac Watts (*History of Dissenters*, pp. 111, 473–4): 'This tendency to philosophize upon matters of pure revelation, forms, indeed, the chief fault in the doctor's writings, and may be traced to his connection with the philosophers and literati of the day, whose suffrage to his sentiments he was desirous to gain.' This should be taken along with the historians' exoneration of Thomas Bradbury, of whom it is reported, in a testimony which they quote, that 'he made it his business not only from his own pulpit, but at the Pinner's-hall lecture, to lampoon and satirize the performances of Dr. Watts, and amongst others his hymns and psalms, for which many Christians and churches have reason to bless God'. Bogue and Bennett comment (p. 494): 'Thomas Bradbury . . . was not the only friend of the Gospel who was prejudiced against the doctor's devotional poetry, and alarmed at the supposed consequences of introducing it into the dissenting worship.' Thus Watts and Hall alike are condemned for having sought the suffrages of 'the literati'.

At such hands Philip Doddridge in his turn could expect to be, at best, damned with faint praise. And so it proves (pp. 482–3):

He was the soul of every association for religious purposes in the country where he resided; for his heart was too large to be confined to Northampton. He was not equally excellent as a divine; for a mistaken candour often destroyed precision of sentiment, and energy of expression. . . . His publications are deficient in vigour, nor can they be said to evince an exuberance of original thought in the author, or force the profitable labour of thinking upon the reader. Yet they are always serious, respectable, and useful.

Such comments on the luminaries of early Hanoverian Dissent sufficiently show why Bennett thirty years later could allude in passing, when speaking of dissenters' preaching, to 'the inanity that prevailed in the reigns of the first princes of the House of Hanover'.

More far-reaching, however – and quite deliberately so, for Bogue and Bennett are no fools – are the implications of ascribing to Doddridge 'a mistaken candour'. What this means, they had spelled out earlier (p. 384):

> The misapplication of the word candour was more injurious in its effects on religious sentiments, than can now be well conceived. It was supposed to possess indescribable virtues. Candour was sounded from many a pulpit; and like charity, it was supposed to hide a multitude of sins. An orthodox minister who had candour, was to believe that an arian or socinian was a very good man; and that if he was sincere in his opinions, and not rigid in condemning others, he ought not to be condemned himself. The influence of this idea was exceedingly pernicious; for it led to an indifference with respect to truth and error, which depraved both their sentiments and dispositions, which relaxed the springs of Christian integrity and conduct, and gradually brought them to call good evil and evil good, to put light for darkness and darkness for light. This was another of the arian idols. Dr. Doddridge, whose softness of temper led him to more intercourse with ministers of the new opinions than most of his brethren, was sensible of the blindness of this boasted candour, and frequently mentions, with considerable feeling, that its possessors could exercise it to all but those who were the ardent believers of evangelical doctrine.

Though Doddridge is thus at this point exonerated, when on a later page he is charged with 'mistaken candour', Bogue and Bennett mean to accuse him of everything that this passage spells out. The proof is at pages 479–80, where they are unsparing in their castigation of 'the spurious liberality' which 'perverted' Doddridge's seminary at Northampton:

> This inattention to the genuine religion of the youths, which we should call the original sin of the institution, poisoned Doddridge's lectures; for they seem to proceed too much on the idea that the mind of the student was a perfect *tabula rasa*, destitute of sentiments or prepossessions. Had this been the case, we could not approve of the tutors furnishing them with the wrong as well as the right in theology, error as well as truth, and then calling them to make their election. If such conduct be defended under the name of liberality, would it not be still more liberal, to admit persons who were yet speculating whether Christianity, deism, or atheism was most consistent with truth?

Here, the substitution of 'liberal' for 'candid' may alert us to the fact that in 1976 this is still a live issue – and by no means only in theology. But in any case Robert Hall, who had decided in 1801 for 'devout, liberal, rational, yet fervent piety, of the stamp of Doddridge, who is now my favourite among divines', could not expect to get favourable treatment from such as Bogue and Bennett, who (unfortunately for him) represented the consensus of dissenting opinion in his lifetime, and the future of dissenting sentiment throughout the nineteenth century. The unbridgeable cleavage between them cannot be more precisely pinpointed than in the way the historians single out themselves – on the issue of 'Candour', that central principle of Enlightenment culture, the one that Bogue and Bennett cannot stomach.

And in fact there is evidence to support their contention that 'candour' was indeed the specious pretext by which the Unitarians contrived to subvert English Dissent from within. Thus their contemporary, Joseph Ivimey (*History of the English Baptists*, 1823, vol. 3, p. 400n.), comments that a Baptist congregation was led to accept the Socinian James Foster as their pastor 'by their false notions of candour and catholicism', and Ivimey reproduces the memorial inscription to Foster, which declares that 'notwithstanding the censures which fell upon him, he was candid towards all whom he believed sincere'. This casts a beam of unintended irony on Anthony Lincoln's judgment that the dissenters' Application to Parliament in 1772, for the repeal of the Toleration Act, 'as a whole, was sincerely what it professed to be: an appeal to "candour"'. This attempt by Unitarians to speak for a body of sentiment which was, as events showed, overwhelmingly Trinitarian was in fact conspicuously 'uncandid', as the eighteenth century understood 'candour'. It is, I suspect, this discreditable manoeuvre more than anything else which brought candour into such disrepute as it had for George Canning, when he inserted his 'New Morality' into the last number of the *Anti-Jacobin* (1798):

> 'Much may be said on both sides,' hark, I hear
> A well-known voice that murmurs in my ear, –
> The voice of Candour. Hail! most solemn sage,
> Thou drivelling virtue of this moral age,
> Candour – which softens party's headlong rage;
> Candour – which spares its foes; nor e'er descends
> With bigot zeal to combat for its friends.
> Candour – which loves in see-saw strain to tell
> Of acting foolishly, but meaning well;
> Too nice to praise by wholesale, or to blame,
> Convinced that all men's motives are the same;
> And finds, with keen discriminating sight,
> Black's not too black, nor white so very white. . . .

The *Anti-Jacobin*, of course, is hardly a disinterested witness. Yet those who in the twentieth century have seen the duplicity of communist and ex-communist intellectuals will recognize readily enough the sort of people whom Canning is exposing and the rhetorical strategies that they commonly employ. What they brought about seems indisputable: by their manoeuvres, 'candour', which had been for a George Berkeley perhaps the cardinal principle of ethics (see my 'Berkeley and the Style of Dialogue' in H. S. Davies and G. Watson (eds), *The English Mind*, 1964), had become by the end of the century a piece of dangerous *cant*.

p. 82 *Arnold . . . supercilious milk-and-water to the assembled clergy of London. . . .*
It is plainly Arnold, in a deplorable performance such as this (though the Arnold of *Culture and Anarchy* also), who angered P. T. Forsyth in 1896:

> Culture, aesthetic or even religious, is now the most deadly and subtle enemy of spiritual freedom. It is the growth of culture in the decay of Gospel that the soul's freedom has increasingly to dread. It is there that our Nonconformity is in most danger of being untrue to itself and its mission. We *are* suffering. But it is less from grievance now than from success. We share a prosperity which is passing through variety of interest, refinement of taste, aesthetic emotion, tender pity, kindly careless catholicity, and over-sweet reasonableness, to leanness of soul. It is more at home in literature than in Scripture, and in journals more than either. And it tends to substitute charity and its sympathies for grace and its faith. These are tendencies of the time which we have not escaped. I cannot measure the extent to which we have been affected by them, I may only say that, if any churches can thrive on them, it [*sic*] is not ours. To us they are not only dangerous, but fatal. Humanism must indeed find a home in grace which it has never occupied yet. But it is another thing when it becomes a church's note.

Were it not for the distinction of Forsyth's language – consider the mordant accuracy of 'in journals more than either' – we might mistake this for the philistinism of Bogue and Bennett ninety years before, or of Spurgeon even as Forsyth was writing. But it is not so. Forsyth presents a true bill not only against Arnold, but also (prophetically) against thinkers of 'the Arnoldian persuasion' into our own day.

The persevering vindictiveness of Arnold's polemic against Dissent is not always recognized. Already, in his *Essays in Criticism*, he had been unable to applaud the pieties of Eugénie de Guérin without immolating an Englishwoman, Emma Tatham, and sneering at her 'union in church-fellowship with the worshippers at Hawley Square Chapel, Margate':

> Both were fervent Christians, and, so far, the two lives have a real resemblance; but, in the setting of them, what a difference! The Frenchwoman is a Catholic in Languedoc; the Englishwoman is a Protestant at Margate; Margate, that brick-and-mortar image of English Protestantism, representing it in all its prose, all its uncomeliness, – let me add, all its salubrity.

William Hale White and Peter Taylor Forsyth deserve credit for picking up the gauntlet thus tauntingly thrown down, not once but many times.

Forsyth (1848–1921), a Congregationalist theologian who deserves some of the credit given to more modish foreign names like Emil Brunner and Karl Barth, is a very interesting case that deserves study from students of English as well as of Theology. In *Christ on Parnassus* (1911), a book much less impressive than his strictly theological works, Forsyth can be seen still arguing with Arnold, without naming him (p. 232):

> It is said sometimes, with a vague grandeur which captivates half culture, that poetry is religion and religion is poetry; and so we have all the realities of faith melted by the sleight and patter of some voluble conjuror into the final fabric of a vision, an airy, unsubstantial pageant of imagination. This is a loose and vicious use of words. Faith, indeed, is incomplete without imagination, and imagination is baseless without faith. But neither can stand for the other, or do its work.

Here, from a dissenting pulpit, we surely have the Arnoldian programme punctured just as it was by T. E. Hulme when he objected to 'poetry as spilt religion', and as it was to be twenty years later when Eliot lectured on Arnold and Pater in his *Use of Poetry and Use of Criticism* (1933). Forsyth goes on:

> it is a salutary feature of religious feeling that it is abandoning the excessive formlessness which it had assumed in the hands of its most liberal and sentimental champions; and it is seeking to recover, if it has not actually found, an historic positivity which shall not be rigidly formal, a shapeliness which shall not be of iron mould, a system which shall be truly and morally rational, and a law which shall steady and shall not stunt its career.

And Forsyth concludes his *rappel à l'ordre* with the utmost trenchancy:

> To say, then, that religion is poetry would really be, if we measured our words, to re-import into religion with salutary vigour that element of definite and eternal form which seemed in danger of passing into a general being as

142

featureless as the sky, and a catholic emotion as facile as the wind. Undog-matic Christianity is mere music; it is not even poetry.

Music lovers may well chafe at this formulation; a poet cannot fail to realize that this emphasis on 'definite and eternal form' gives to poetry a dignity beyond anything that we find in Matthew Arnold.

Notes to Lecture 6

I quote Jessie Chambers from E. Delavenay, *D. H. Lawrence et la génèse de son oeuvre*, 1969, vol. 2, appendix 4, pp. 695–6. Sybil Wingate's memoir appeared first in the *Spectator* for 29 May 1959, and is repro-duced by Derek Tulloch, *Wingate in Peace and War* (1972). 'The devil raged against the boy preacher' is quoted from Ernest W. Bacon, *Spurgeon: Heir of the Puritans*, 1967, p. 50. For A. L. Rowse, see *Appeasement: A Study in Political Decline 1933–39*, 1961, p. 19.

Index

146

149